The Shadow
of the Cross

A Journey Through the Virtues
of Celtic Spirituality

Monsignor Eric R. Barr

ACTA

ASSISTING CHRISTIANS TO ACT

PUBLICATIONS

The Shadow of the Cross
A Journey Through the Virtues of Celtic Spirituality
by Monsignor Eric R. Barr, STL

Edited by Andrew Yankech
Cover design and photo by Tom A. Wright
Typesetting by Desktop Edit Shop, Inc.

Scripture quotations are from the *New Revised Standard Version of the Bible,* copyright © 1989 by the Division of Christian Education of the National Council of the Churches of Christ in the U.S.A. Used with permission. All rights reserved.

Copyright © 2004 by Msgr. Eric R. Barr

Published by: ACTA Publications
                  Assisting Christians to Act
                  4848 N. Clark Street
                  Chicago, IL 60640
                  773-271-1030
                  www.actapublications.com
                  actapublications@aol.com

Library of Congress Number: 2003115217
ISBN: 0-87946-262-0
Printed in the United States of America
Year: 10 09 08 07 06 05 04
Printing: 10 9 8 7 6 5 4 3 2 1

Contents

Therefore let us concern ourselves with heavenly things, not human ones, and like pilgrims always sigh for our homeland. Because we are travelers and pilgrims through this world, it is the road's end, that is of our lives, that we should always be thinking about. So while we are on the road as guests of the world, let us fill our minds with heavenly and spiritual things: our theme song, "When shall I come and appear before the face of my God?"

St. Columbanus (Sermon 8)

Introduction

I f you are a couch potato, this book may not be for you. Of course, if you are given to action rather than reflection, this book may not be for you either. However, if you think life is a journey and if you think that where and how you walk in life is important, then maybe it's worth your while to read a little further. Think of this book as a primer of Celtic spiritual aerobics with tips on how to walk a spiritual path and exercises on how to keep fit, whole and healthy along the way. And while you are deciding whether or not such a journey is for you, read this story about an Irish lad, a person just like us. It is stark, poignant, decisive, compelling, and it's all true.

For a long time, he had heard the whisper in his heart, the words once spoken to Abraham:"Leave your own country and your kinfolk, and your Father's house, and come to the land I will show you...." For a long time, she who was his mother had seen the signs: the hours of prayer, the restlessness of her son. And she remembered the dream that visited her before his birth, how a brilliant sun arose from her breast and illuminated the world. Everything came to a head that evening as the twilight faded. "I'm leaving," he said. "You mustn't!" she replied. He picked up a lightly packed bag and moved to the door. She threw her body across the threshold, begging him not to leave kith and kin, hearth and home. "Do not grieve me," he said, and then without another word, he stepped across her body on the threshold, walked out the door and never looked back as he strode out upon the road under a canopy of burning stars.[1]

The young man's name was Columbanus, and before we think too harshly of him for abandoning his mother, hear why the story was told in the first place. Whether or not he was a good son was immaterial and unknown: That was not the point of the tale. What was most important was what he was doing. He was taking to the road, not as a directionless vagrant, but as a restless wanderer for Christ. It was a call from God heard often by the youth of sixth century Ireland. In that time, the threshold of a doorway was a sacred space: a place in between places, where wondrous things could happen. The fact that his mother also occupied that same space as Columbanus stepped over both threshold and parent is even more portentous. He was leaving everything for God. He was living the Gospel-call of Christ: "No one who puts a hand to the plow and looks back is fit for the Kingdom of God." (Luke 9:62)[2]

It is said that Columbanus never looked back, not out of coldness or callousness, but because he was changed. His destiny had been given to him, and nothing could come in the way of his fulfillment of that charge from Christ: to wander the world preaching the Gospel, spreading the message of the Lord of Lords. While he took many highways and paths along the way, the spiritual road he walked led straight to the Blessed Lands where the Holy Ones of God and the Son of Heaven dwell, a place you and I know as heaven. Being a wanderer for Christ was not an aimless task. It was quite the opposite, really. It was knowing you were traveling directly to God regardless of where the hand of God directed you.

From Ireland, Columbanus traveled to the continent of Europe, a land floundering in the swampy twilight of the Dark Ages. We can follow his route still, through the modern countries of France and Switzerland, Germany and Italy. In a time of violence and superstition, he and his companions were a light in the darkness. Because they knew the spiritual road, that path to God the heart seeks, they brought others to the truth. Because the inner map of their soul was carefully charted, they steered barbarians to knowledge and helped a chaotic Europe return to the order of civilization.

Columbanus' quest for spiritual enlightenment is a familiar one to all cultures. The quest for meaning is not the province of any one particular faith. But Columbanus and those nameless others who, fifteen hundred years ago, spread from Ireland back into Europe to re-Christianize that shattered land, did two things unusual in humanity's search for meaning.

First, they realized that spirituality is a quest, a journey, a road of sorrow and a way of joy. Columbanus once said, "We are all guests of the world," meaning that our true home lies elsewhere. Our quest is toward something or someone. It is actually a journey with a concrete goal in mind. No matter how winding the road, how tortuous the path, Christ is the destination—not self-actualization, enlightenment or personal well-being. Of course, for Columbanus and the others, when they found Christ, they found everything, including who they were and why they were even alive.

What is unique here is not the journey aspect, but the fact that even before the journey starts the quest is clear: Find Christ and be his companion. In many modern versions of the spiritual quest, vague and abstract concepts of ultimate meaning are the road signs on the journey of life. Among those who believe in a plethora of gods, goddesses or spiritual forces, the focus of the quest is to find which divine mentor should guide them and give them meaning. But the Celtic Christian already knows where he or she is going. The journey is a surrender to the will of God and a purifying of one's own humanity. That stands apart from other spiritual quests. In Native American religions one often goes on a purifying journey to find a spirit totem or guide, not really sure what divine *manitou* or spirit will manifest itself. In Eastern religions, the spiritual journey is towards enlightenment but without a clear knowledge of what that enlightenment will bring. These forms of spiritual journeys are akin to getting in a car for a road trip and driving east. The big city is over there beyond the hills, and though we're not quite certain how to get there, we'll see what happens on the way. This is not the Christian way of journeying on the spiritual path. We know clearly where we are going, and while it is true that many unexpected events will happen on the journey, we wish to see Jesus. Jesus is the only destination we have.

The second unusual thing that marks Celtic Christianity as unique is this: Columbanus, and those like him, knew that the road they walked was not a lonely one. It was a spiritual road sunk smack dab in the midst of the world with all its beauty and its darkness. They could no more withdraw from the world than a fish could forsake the water. It was essential to live their lives in the context of the times they found themselves in.

The Celtic Christian never walks alone. This spirituality is infused with the knowledge that each one of us is linked by our belief in Christ. It is fundamentally *ecclesially* oriented. In other words, this spirituality lives and breathes within a community, a church. The popularization of Celtic Christianity has led some to posit an opposition between Celtic and Roman Christianity. While arguments did occur, they were never serious enough to cause an actual break. There were never two churches—one Celtic, one Roman. The Irish saints who re-Christianized Europe deeply felt their connection to the city of Rome with its bones of Peter and Paul: apostles and tangible links to Christ. All maintained great esteem for the successor of those apostles, namely the Bishop of Rome, the Pope.

In the midst of the foggy darkness that dampened the continent and the light of Christ that burned brightly in Celtic Britain and Ireland, most people were only too glad to grasp the thread of history that linked their mission of evangelization with the two great apostles to the world, Peter and Paul. That bond of history and faith brought Christians together in a human church that breathed the Divine Presence in the sacraments and a shared history. Rome, for its part, treasured these Celtic monks, who brought fresh life into a beleaguered faith. That is the beauty of Celtic spirituality: It enlivens our faith by giving us a new look at the dynamic and all-encompassing message of the Gospel. The flexibility and creativity of Celtic spirituality shows the importance of individual prayer, but it is always linked to the greater community of the Church. Columbanus, that great Dark Ages missionary of light, and his Celtic monks show clearly that the spiritual path is not just interior: It affects others and brings them closer to Christ. What, then, makes this particular way of walking the spiritual path unique? Celtic spirituality focuses on Christ as the goal of the journey and the fact that there is no such thing as a solitary Christian. As individuals we all have a need for a community of worshippers in contact with the Divine. Our spiritual journey affects others just as their journeys affect us.

Formed during the Golden Age of Ireland's early Christian era and matured in the midst of Europe's Dark Ages, Celtic spirituality stands as a fitting paradigm for Christians at the dawn of the third millennium. It is a spirituality refreshingly free of self-centeredness, free of esoteric secrets and mysteries, and amazingly untouched by spiritual approaches, popular today, which either reject the world as a lie or an illusion, or accept that world as all there is.

It would be easy to think of Celtic spirituality as the newest fad, or the only spiritual method we should practice. Nothing could be further from the truth. It is simply a way to walk the road of life, and if you find it helpful, that is enough. Take it all, or take it in bits and pieces, whatever you need to help you journey on your road.

Now for the controversial part. No one can walk the road of life without commitment. It is a curious and perhaps spiritually fatal fallacy of our age that there are many truths and any spiritual path is as good as the next one. "What is most important," say the modern sages, "is that you are journeying." That sentiment, however, treats faith, religion and the practice of spirituality much as a supermarket treats consumer products: One is as good as the other, it all depends on the wish of the consumer. In business, that makes sense; in spirituality, it creates chaos. Not all paths lead to the truth. Commitment to a spiritual path means accepting something as more true than something else. There are many spiritual methods, Celtic spirituality being one of them. But truth is truth, and in the Christian scheme of things all truths by definition lead to Christ, for he is "the Way, the Truth, the Life." Why walk a road that ends in the jungle or only leads to the suburbs; why not walk the road that leads to the heart of the city? For those baptized in Christ, Jesus is the source and goal. There can be no other. This is important, particularly in the Celtic spiritual way of walking this journey. Columbanus and those who followed him loved the continental Christians, many of whom had lapsed back into the ways of paganism, but Columbanus and his followers never tolerated the return to the ancient gods. Truth was truth, and Pan was a poor substitute for the God who created the forests and fields in which the so-called pagan gods were supposed to have frolicked. The Celtic monks who re-Christianized Europe were not content to leave people wallowing in half-truths, for half-truths are also half-falsehoods.

Celtic spirituality has a confidence and a trust in the essential truth of the Christian message. While it respects the truth found in other religions, it does so in the context that such truths will lead the seeker to Jesus. Authentic Celtic spirituality is not going to be a comfortable place for those who take refuge in ambiguity, thinking that the spiritual journey is more important than the truth it is based on. Celtic spirituality will not allow a person to strip the supernatural of its power by stating that all interpretations of it are to be applauded and accepted. Channeling, crystal gazing, astrology and other forms of occult activity are scorned by Celtic spirituality, and indeed by all forms of Christian spirituality, not because of their ineffectiveness, but because of their power to take people on a road away from Christ, away from Truth.

Despite the above, Celtic spirituality is not intolerant. It realizes that truth can exist in other paths, even in paganism. While the fullness of God's truth rests in Christianity, God does not restrict his light solely to Christianity. To hold that Christianity is the fullest expression of God's revelation says less about other religions' deficiencies and everything about the absolute commitment the Christian makes to Jesus. Celtic spirituality has a unique ability to transform the imperfect visions of other spiritual paths and use the truth present there to enhance the Christian message. The peaceful conversion of Ireland in the fifth century was not without conflict, but ultimately the pagan priests, the Druids of that land, became the Christian priests of the new religion because Christianity converted them by convincing them of its truth. Without a single case of martyrdom, Ireland shifted from paganism to Christianity. In a way more gentle than in other parts of the world, conversion happened because the presence of Christ was already there and his message understood, albeit imperfectly, in the way the inhabitants of Ireland lived their lives and perceived the Divine. Christianity took what was good and pointed out the essential Christ-ness of it. For instance, holy wells once sacred to pagan gods are now known by the names of holy saints whose Christianity revealed more clearly the presence of God in those sacred spaces. Sacred times of the year lost their dedication to the gods who represented forces of nature and instead became associated with Christ, St.

Brigid and St. Michael the Archangel, because those who preached this new Christian faith gave a better understanding of the holiness of the seasons. Why light a fire to the god Lugh in springtime, a god whom you never met, when you could light the Easter fire in honor of the Christ, the God with the human face, whom you could receive each week in the Eucharist?

Even this sentiment sounds triumphalistic and arrogant to those of this age who suffer from the paralysis of ambiguity. Throwing up their hands, they wrap themselves in the blandness of indecision. Call it what you will—secularism, humanism, agnosticism, even "Christianity-lite"—this paralysis of ambiguity has effectively shut off large numbers of people of all denominations and religions from the active pursuit of truth.

In this confusing time, Celtic spirituality serves as a refreshing splash of cool water on the collective face of the modern world. When so many people have adopted the view that reality is in the eye of the beholder and that each individual ultimately makes up his or her own truth, this spirituality offers a no-nonsense look at Christianity and how to live that message in daily life. Most importantly, it helps a person experience the dynamic God who created the world and continually demonstrates a parental love for each human being and creature. That possibility of encounter with the Divine may make this a spirituality for you.

May this book serve as a reliable map on this journey of life, this road of sorrow and way of joy, that takes place for all of us in the shadow of the cross.

HOW TO USE THIS BOOK

Prayer involves the whole person: body, mind and spirit. Nobody needs to be a saint in order to pray. My mother tells the story of my father bringing home each newborn child (there were six of us) and laying that baby on the bed, unwrapping all the blankets, and simply looking at the child in all its pink, healthy innocence. Then he would pronounce the baby beautiful. He would thank God for the gift and hold his wife as they marveled over what they had accomplished. Though he would not have phrased it this way, what he was doing was prayer: He held a great truth in his mind (the fact of a newborn child); he immersed himself in that truth (the time he spent marveling at the child); he responded and conversed with God (his thanks to the Creator for this new child and the gift of marriage and parenthood). Behold, immerse, respond—that is prayer in its totality. We behold through story. We immerse by reflection. We respond by meditative, contemplative and active prayer. A college degree in spirituality or a course in prayer technique is not needed, just a willingness to reflect on the important matters of life and converse with God.

The following chapters are meant to stand each on their own, so feel free to skip around and pick the ones that speak to you now in your life. Taken together, though, they present the basics of our faith—not through catechism, but through prayer.

Each chapter is divided into three parts, which correspond to the three parts that make up prayer in its totality:

1. **A story from the Celtic Tradition:** When we read stories of the Celtic saints or hear of Celtic Christian traditions, we come face to face with the Divine. Whether it is a story of

Patrick battling the Druids in a test of truth, Brigid taking care of a humble leper, or Columba talking with his favorite horse, God shines through, bringing to us a profound truth that can touch our lives and point us more surely on our spiritual path. We behold this truth in the context of a story, and because the story is brief and complete we can hold the entire story in our mind with its images, actions and messages.

2. **A reflection on the story:** Stories are just stories until we immerse ourselves in them, and since these stories deeply touch the human heart we will spend some time reflecting on their meaning. The reflection is not exhaustive. These stories have lasted a long time precisely because of their ability to carry deep truths. It is impossible to exhaust their riches.

3. **A response to God:** Everyone's response to God is different, but some ideas and questions are given to point us all on our way.

Don't be a slave to the process. The above points are simply guidelines. Make these stories your own and let them lead you to a newer, fresher understanding of what it means to be a follower of Christ.

Packing for the Trip

Fifteen hundred years ago, when things Celtic and Christian were just getting started, many men and women lived in group communities known as monasteries. Not as formal as the monasteries of our day, they were the centers of Irish civilization. Other family groups, smiths, market places and schools would gather around them. Monks and nuns of the monasteries would busy themselves with hours of prayer, work in the community, and private study. They were definitely in the world, but they needed to get back often to their spiritual roots and redirect themselves on their journey of life. They would consequently go out in solitude to the forest or field or plant themselves on some lonely cliff above the sea to re-orient themselves. Here's a little poem by one of them, the focus of meditation for this chapter:

> *Grant me, sweet Christ, the grace to find, Son of the*
> *   Living God,*
> *A small hut in a lonesome spot*
> *To make my abode.*
>
> *A little pool but very clear, to stand beside the place*

Where every sin is washed away
By sanctifying grace.

A pleasant woodland all about, to shield it from
*   the wind*
And make a home for singing birds
Before it and behind.

A southern aspect for the heat, a stream along
*   its foot*
A smooth green lawn with rich topsoil
Propitious to all fruit.

My choice of those to live with me and pray to God
*   as well;*
Quiet friends of humble mind
Their number I shall tell.

A lovely church, a home for God, bedecked with
*   linen fine,*
Where o'er the whitened Gospel page
The Gospel candle shine.

A little house where all may dwell, and body's care
*   be sought,*
Where none shows lust or arrogance,
None thinks an evil thought.

And all I ask for housekeeping I get and pay
     no fees,
Leeks from the garden, poultry, game,
Salmon, fruit and bees.

My share of clothing and of food from the King of
     fairest face,
And I to sit at times alone
And pray in every place.[3]

⟡

Think of the last time you moved or went on a vacation. There were so many decisions. Moves and vacations are important because they teach us that we can live with quite a bit less than we think. They force us to jettison the non-essentials so that we can focus on the matter at hand, whether that be a new job, a new home or a new place to visit. In this time of wealth and material prosperity, where even bad economic times mean we do with a little less rather than with nothing, the virtue of **detachment** may seem awfully spartan and out of touch with the times. Why shouldn't we partake in the latest technology, have the best car, the most beautiful furniture? These are things God has made through the hands of others and placed in our lives to make existence easier and more enjoyable.

All major faiths will tell us that it is better to *be* than to *do*. Most of the possessions we want, however, help us more with *doing* things than with *being* ourselves. While it is great to have computers and Internet access, cell phones and instant communication, and utensils that take the "work" out of work, we get so enmeshed in *doing* that we lose ourselves. We cannot hear our heart because of the tumultuous activity all around us. Constantly on the go, we are never still.

Notice what we do with our children. Added to all the other duties of parenting is the task of chauffeuring one child to this game, that one to music lessons, the soccer kid to scouts after the game, the budding Beethoven to swim class after the music lesson. Somewhere in the future that child, now an aged grandparent, will muse, "I remember my mom. She was the lady in the front seat of the car who took me to McDonald's in between my games and music lessons." It seems that in our age most in-depth family conversations now happen in the car between activities—not around the family dinner table.

Parents are still good parents—they are just busier. We are still good individuals despite the brave new world we live in. But relentless, unending activity has drowned out the voice of God, who comes to us more often like the still, small voice Elijah heard on Mount Horeb than the towering pillar of cloud of the Exodus.

Even Celtic Christians of millennia ago knew the dangers of allowing oneself to be possessed by the world. The world is not bad, but we were meant to be masters of it, not its subjects. Sometimes it does seem that the things we have created, these things of earth, rule us. When that happens all people on the journey of life have to pause and take stock. The Celtic monks knew that they needed to strip away the chains. That is why they separated from the busy world and re-established priorities.

Their innate common sense did not make them fly to church, cast themselves before the Cross, and cry, "The world is bad; only God is good!" They simply stepped away for a while, got away from the clutter, and remembered God. That's how they re-energized and found the strength to step again into the world, aware of God and focused on what truly matters.

The monk in the little poem above wants a house, nature, a church and good food and water. He wants the basics, but in such a way that he has time to be with God. That was easy for him to do, living in a time and culture that made such a lifestyle viable. But what about us? How do we detach from the world in a normal and healthy way?

It's simple, really. Detachment is all about setting priorities. If God is number one in our lives, everything else falls into place. Of course, it is easy to *say* God comes first. In fact, we do that all the time in our culture. The Gallup Organization, famous for its periodic polls, shows belief in God to be supremely high in the United States: over ninety-seven percent of Americans believe in God. Sounds like God is number one, right? Not so fast. A closer look reveals that God seems to be a movable concept, good to believe in but not so important in our daily lives. Over forty percent say they worship God each week, but other studies say the reality is closer to twenty-six percent. Critics may claim that attendance at church is not a prerequisite for believing in God, but this simple weekly act can provide a convenient and regular break from our normal, hectic schedules, a set time each week to recharge our spiritual batteries.[4]

So where does God fall in most people's lives? For many of us God trails somewhere behind television, kids, spouse, friends and work. Nearly everybody and everything gets more time during the day than God. Even personal hygiene, eating and dressing ourselves get a higher portion of our time than God.

This does not make us bad people, but realizing this ought to make us honest. Jesus said, "For where your treasure is, there your heart will be also." (Matthew 6:21) We proclaim our priorities by what we do. We cannot claim friendship with a God to whom we seldom speak. Because of our busy schedules we have an acquaintanceship with God, but not a deep friendship.

We may take solace in the fact that, if God is not number one then most probably family and work probably are, and those are certainly worthy commitments, right? Absolutely. But that still presents a problem. Our God says they *cannot* be number one. God said to Moses, "I am the Lord your God, you shall have no strange gods before me," meaning that anything that takes precedence over, God is really another god and this is not allowable. Jesus also says, "You shall love the Lord your God with all your heart, and with all your soul, and with all your mind, and with all your strength, [and] you shall love your neighbor as yourself." (Mark 12:30-31) This means that God must be number one, but people, especially families, had better be number two. Detachment is about keeping our eyes on the road. If we are too busy with the sights and sounds along the side of the road, we might miss what is right in front of us, or worse, we can go crashing off the road in an accident that keeps us from traveling on a straight path to God.

The complexity of our modern world seems to hinder our pursuit of a stronger spiritual path. With all the other obligations we have, do we really have time for an hour of daily prayer or real time alone with God? When we think about what the spiritual life entails, it seems like one more burden among the many we already carry.

Again, Celtic detachment is a virtue that helps with this common barrier to spiritual progress. It is really a positive, not a negative, concept. It is not so much about giving up luxuries or possessions as it is about setting priorities. For instance, what if I look at my life and say, "God isn't number one in my life." If I say that and decide to make God my top priority, then I had better have concrete actions to back that up.

In the early days of Celtic spirituality monks had a little "desert" to go to—an out of the way place, usually a forest hut or a cleft in a rocky hillside. They could go there often to refocus their lives on God. No such luck for us. Modern life does not permit this opportunity. We have to compromise creatively. We have to create a sacred space, a sacred time for ourselves that we can go to and focus on God, to step away from complexity and hear the silence in our hearts and hope to hear the voice of Christ.

We do not need much. For myself, it helps to paraphrase those ancient Celtic verses at the beginning of this chapter thus:

Jesus, my friend and Lord, I would love to have a
place where I could go, somewhere away from
the busy-ness of my life, a place I could call
home;

A place by some water, a place where I could hear
the waves or just the running of a stream, clear
water to remind me of my baptism;

And then a bright woodland full of birds that sing
in the leaf-shadowed sunlight;

A place to plant a garden, fertile soil to grow the
flowers I love and the food that graces my table;

A church or a chapel nearby, a home for you, my
Lord, beautiful in silence and peace,

And enough clothing and food to satisfy only my
needs, so that I could sit a while and pray to you
my God wherever I would be.

The yearning for a home away from home is natural to the human being. In our secular world we refer to it as "getting away." But what we really want is some truth to fill the spiritual vacuum inside us. The sacred space does not have to be large. The sacred time can be brief. What matters is that there is a place and time dedicated to God. You should make sure your goal is achievable, though. If you only pray about five minutes a day now, try increasing it to ten or fifteen. Just remember that nothing should come between you and that sacred time. That's what making God your number one priority means. Many people on a spiritual quest start out with unrealistic goals. Be sensible. Of course ten minutes a day is not going to elevate God to your top priority, but time is not the only standard: Intent matters too. A little change like this means ten minutes less of something else, and since we shouldn't necessarily decrease our time with family or work, it will most likely be less TV, or golf, or some other leisure activity. By cutting back on some of our unnecessary luxuries, we can gradually re-orient ourselves toward God.

One of the things Catholics are discovering in their lives is how easy it is to give up Sunday Mass. Many well-meaning Catholics have placed this time into a second, third or fourth priority level. "I will go to Mass if there is not a soccer game, shopping to do, etc." The truth, however, is that after a while something always seems to come up, Mass attendance is no longer regular, and God is no longer number one. Detachment is a matter of priorities. Making God our most important priority is the first step to a stronger spiritual life. Celtic Christianity makes detachment a basic building block for spiritual progress.

Meditation

The story of St. Columbanus in the introduction strikes most people as very harsh. How could you step over your own mother and never look back? And yet this seemingly callous and even brutal action demonstrates the same value of detachment as the more gentle and pastoral poem at the beginning of this chapter. Detachment means letting go and setting priorities. On a piece of paper, write down the five most important people, tasks or things you value. Hopefully God will be there, but if not, make God number six. For each item jot down the ways you keep this person, task or thing important in your life. For instance, if sports is a top priority you might write, "I read the sports page every morning; I play fantasy football at the office; etc." Or if your family is important, you might say, "I spend time with the kids each night; my spouse and I spend ten minutes of quality time talking over the day; etc." After you are done, look the paper over. Where does God really fit in your life? What needs to be done in order to make your Creator number one?

Contemplation

Meditation is a busy prayer activity, but contemplation means resting in the presence of the Lord. In the meditation you reflected on the place God holds in your life. Whatever that result, come before the Lord as you are. Go to a quiet place and spend ten minutes simply surrendering yourself to God. The aspiration "Jesus, my Lord, my God, my all," is a good phrase to use to gently focus your attention on God. Don't worry if you get distracted. The point is that you've promised these ten minutes to the Lord. They are your gift to him, your detachment from the complexity of every day.

Action

This week resolve to do one action that will demonstrate your willingness to make your relationship with God your top priority. Be sensible. Set your sights on an action you can actually achieve. Some suggestions: a promise to pray at midday for a minute; a promise to visit a church or adoration chapel at lunchtime once a week; a promise to say the rosary in the car, train or bus while going to work; a promise to be more enthusiastic as Sunday worship rolls around and to communicate that enthusiasm to friends or family members.

The Celtic Virtue of Awareness

The Elusive God

And the time finally arrived when Patrick of the clear voice and great heart met the High King of Ireland. It happened on the Vigil of Easter, before the Easter fire blazing in the dark on the Hill of Slane opposite the High King's stronghold of Tara. The King ordered Patrick to appear before him at dawn. Ominous was the meeting to the Druids, the pagan priests and priestesses of the land's religion and people. They feared this new God and new faith. And so the High King withdrew, but the Druids plotted, "We will kill this Patrick as he walks to Tara. We will ambush him in the mist that comes with the dawn." And the Druids lay in wait for Patrick, their long knives ready along the forest path to Tara. At dawn Patrick and his companions began the walk to Tara of the High Kings. But the saint sensed danger, smelled the evil intentions of the Druids ahead of him, ready to kill him on the forest path. He raised his head to where the sun was soon to rise and he began to sing a hymn of protection. And this is what he sang:

> *In this fateful hour,*
> *I place all heaven with its power,*
> *And the sun with its brightness,*
> *And the snow with its whiteness,*
> *And the fire with all the strength it hath,*

And the lightning with its rapid wrath,
And the winds with their swiftness along the path,
And the sea with its deepness,
And the rocks with their steepness,
And the earth with its starkness,
All these I place,
By God Almighty's help and grace,
Between myself and the powers of darkness!

I bind unto myself this day,
The strong name of the Trinity,
By invocation of the same,
The Three in One,
And One in Three.

Christ be with me, Christ within me,
Christ behind me, Christ before me,
Christ beside me, Christ to win me,
Christ to comfort and restore me.
Christ beneath me, Christ above me,
Christ in quiet, Christ in danger,
Christ in the hearts of all that love me,
Christ in the mouth of friend and stranger.[5]

The world was hushed; time stood still; a great silence descend-
ed over the land. Along the forest floor a mist rose up, white as
the pure snow, and hid Patrick and his followers. All the evil
Druids saw through the mist were figures that looked like a
stag leading several deer. Under this disguise, protected by God,

Patrick reached Tara. The rest is another story, but on that East-
er morn, Christ himself claimed Ireland as his own.[6]

THE LORICA OF ST. PATRICK

A Celtic Christian would probably never have understood the modern Christian's complaint: "I don't have time to pray." All times were prayer times for the Celtic Christian. That was a holdover from their pagan roots that taught them that all time is sacred time. The supernatural and the real world were so close that they often intersected in sacred wells and holy hills, forests of oaks and towering stones.

Tucked away in the west of Ireland is St. Brigid's Well, up in County Clare near the windswept shores of the sea. As with many holy sites in Celtic lands, the sacred shares space with the ordinary. Next to a country pub, this roadside shrine seems tiny until one steps into the enclosure. Encompassed by a little cave and wooded knoll, St. Brigid's Well still holds the ability to evoke the power of nature and the presence of the Divine. In the cave is the well itself, and all around the walls of the cave are pictures and prayers of pilgrims who have come to St. Brigid's holy well to pray. Votive offerings in the form of tiny little pieces of red and white rag are tied to the flowering branches that overhang an opening in the cave. It's a custom one sees throughout the land at the holy wells, a little reminder for the saint so that you know your petition was heard.

In places like this it is customary to do the stations—not the

Stations of the Cross but the Celtic stations peculiar to that place. These stations are nothing more or less than a series of prayers and movements meant to involve the whole person in prayer. At St. Brigid's Well it involves traversing the knoll clockwise, kneeling at the cross, and stopping at the well itself, all the while praying a series of traditional prayers. Flowing water, woodland, and the signs of religious devotion mark this clearly as a holy place. Even though it is right by the side of the road, all sound is muffled and the pilgrim is surrounded by God, the saint, and the feeling that all is right with the world. It is a shadow of what it must have been in Eden, when God and humanity walked together in the gentle breeze of the evening.

When Christians came to convert the people of Ireland they liked this attitude of seeing God in the everyday and encouraged the Celts to keep that awareness. They did. The Celts had a great insight, but the beauty of Christianity is that it has always been able to take the insights of human beings and fine tune them, pointing them towards the One Truth. That beautiful gift of seeing the Divine in the world and in the everyday activity around them was made even more awesome by the gift the Christians gave the Celts: awareness of the one, true God.

After the events of the story of St. Patrick above, Ireland turned to Christianity swiftly and without a single martyr. Why was this? A principle reason is that the Druids never really went away. They simply converted. Patrick's expression of God as Trinity, three persons in one God, struck a chord of agreement in the religious thought of the Druids. This idea of God as Trinity helped the Celts take a step up from their pagan religious outlook. It was not that they jettisoned their previous religious experience; they re-interpreted it, seeing it with new understanding.

What makes the Celtic religious experience so appealing is the centrality of the Trinity. For most of us, the dry, dusty saying, "The Trinity is Three Persons in One God," is little more than a hollow formula. We have become what the ancients called *monists*: believers in a static God with no real understanding of how there could be a Father, Son and Holy Spirit. Before this becomes too theological of a discussion, think of your own experience of God. Is God distant? Is God involved in your life? Is God active in the world? For many contemporary people, God is simply a force, like some vague divinity in a science-fiction movie. God is distant, benevolent. We want God to be more, we just don't think it is really possible. This is where the Celts give us a shot in the arm of religious experience.

The reason why the Druids and the Celts liked the Trinity is precisely because the concept represented a God who is *active, involved* and *intimate* with the people and with the world. This is a dynamic God, not some celestial entity. A Greek word captures this Celtic idea perfectly: *perichoresis*, that is, the dance of God. The dynamic relationship between Father, Son and Holy Spirit gives us One God who moves with love, power and interaction with all creation. God is a community of Persons, in which each Person contains, interpenetrates, and dwells in the other two in one magnificent motion of divine love. Without an understanding of this relationship of love between the Three Persons of the Trinity—this "Dance of God"—divinity becomes an abstract concept. We would still think of God as the supreme being, but who would really want to have a relationship with an impersonal force, a static presence, an intellectual concept?

Much of traditional Celtic prayer is done in the name of the Trinity. Christianity gave the Celts a way of looking at God that allowed them to experience God even more closely than they did before. So many things follow from knowing that God is intimately in touch with his creation. This awareness of God gives rise to a belief that miracles can happen, which in this case is the belief that God can reach into our lives and make his presence felt in real and tangible ways. The Celts were not credulous, they just believed that the spiritual world and the real world coexisted in the same universe. Knowing that God is here with us tends to break down our modern idea of the real world being separated from things on a spiritual plane. How can there be much of a difference between the natural and supernatural when God is constantly involved with us?

There are many stories of the Irish saints chatting familiarly not only with the animals of creation but with their own angel companions. A cursory reading of these stories would make the cynic among us say that angels were conjured up at a moment's notice to enhance the legend's charm. But a closer examination of the tradition behind these stories tells a different tale. There are too many accounts of saints talking naturally and amiably with angels, who in these stories are magnificently and distinctly non-human entities, for us to disregard the reality of the situation. Whatever the accuracy of these particular stories, the people who told them, and for whom they were told, believed from experience that such things were normal and natural in a holy person's life.

Celtic Christianity reinforces the awareness that God is everywhere, while reminding people that God is not everything, and this *awareness of God* is key to the Celtic tradition. Do we walk through our daily lives constantly aware of the presence of God? Generally, no. We're too busy. We know we are in trouble when we start saying things like, "I've had a hard day; I'm too tired to pray." In this whole book, prayer will never be named as a virtue. That's because its presence is presumed to be the heart and soul of Celtic Christianity. All times are prayer times.

Celtic prayer is comprised of three characteristics:

1. **Simplicity:** Celtic prayer is made up of heartfelt words of praise and petition devoid of sentimentality and cliché.
2. **Friendship with God:** The Celts grew up with kings and leaders who were of them not above them. That is why Christ, the Chief of Chiefs, is so intimate with the Celt. Their kings and leaders were respected and honored, but not remote. The same is true of the Celtic experience with God. A Christian imbued with Celtic spirituality feels loved by, and at home with, a God who has given each person an important destiny.
3. **A true belief in the power of prayer:** Prayer for the Celtic sensibility is not a last refuge but the first line in the battle between good and evil. Far from being the last thing attempted when all is lost, prayer is seen as essential in confronting any danger and solving any problem.

One of the best ways to see this in action is to look at a type of prayer developed by the Celts. It is called the *Lorica* or Breastplate Prayer. One of the finest Celtic spirituality writers, John J. O'Riordan, tells us "the prayer form takes its origins from St. Paul's image of putting on the spiritual armor of the Lord (Ephesians 10:6-20). It is a prayer of clothing oneself to do battle with the enemy. Hence the term *Lorica* (Breastplate)."[7] The *Lorica* is a strong prayer because those who pray it realize that there is a force in the world opposed to God. While not equal to God, this force, which we call "evil," is personified by Satan. He hates us as much as he hates God. Evil will try to harm us, thus the need for protection. "St. Patrick's *Lorica*," quoted at the beginning of this chapter, is a great example of this type of prayer. No one who prays it can mistake the fact that the composer knew and appreciated the power of his words. It is recognition of the power of God and God's willingness to act in the world on behalf of his people. Trinitarian in nature, it reminds the person who prays that God is with him or her, stronger than evil, and able to protect the petitioner. The *Lorica* is an excellent example of how a person who is truly aware of God ought to pray.

Meditation

One of the most common ways Christians have viewed the purpose of their lives is through the concept of *spiritual warfare.* As tremendously violent as that may sound, the concept is supremely scriptural. In fact, there is a whole gospel dedicated to it: the Gospel of Luke. In the other gospels, the apostles are portrayed as ignorant (Mark); the people, the Jewish leaders and the Roman authorities are Christ's enemies (Matthew); and plots against Jesus abound (John). But Luke is different. Everyone, even Jesus' enemies, are portrayed in a kinder light. They are held in thrall to the power of the evil one; Satan is the enemy. The Adversary of God is the real villain who influences the mortal world.

Luke tells us that after tempting Christ in the desert, "the devil departed to await another opportunity." Christ's death on the cross appeared to be that opportunity, but instead it became the means of our redemption. The Gospel of Luke is the gospel most concerned with mercy, forgiveness and healing, precisely because it recognizes this spiritual warfare. For the Christian, the whole purpose of the spiritual life is to avoid evil, do good, and embrace Christ as Savior. The well-adjusted Christian knows that his or her soul is a battleground. It's not simply the weakness of human nature that gives us faults and failings; it is the temptation and influence of evil as well. The prayer form known as the *Lorica* attempts to recognize this fact and deal with it in reality. Think of your own life for a moment. What battles are you fighting? What evil seeks to weigh you down? How do you fight temptation? Is life a battleground of good and evil for you? If not, why not? Think about the times you have succeeded in fighting evil either in the world or within yourself. What made you successful?

Contemplation

Pick a brief traditional prayer that you know well, or do the action section first and use the prayer you compose. As you pray allow the prayer to surround you. In this "spiritual bubble," protected from all that is outside you, rest in the presence of the Lord. Know that the Lord is there to protect you from evil. Give yourself at least fifteen minutes to pray, but do not keep track of time. The point is that you wish to spend a significant period of time with the Lord.

Action

First, write your own *Lorica*. Follow the steps below.

1. The prayer must be directed to the Trinity: Father, Son and Holy Spirit. Begin and end the prayer by addressing the Lord in this way. Remember that to praise God as Trinity is to call to mind the active nature of God. The very idea of Trinity—God who is love in action—draws us into the divine life of God. Keeping our prayer focused on Father, Son and Holy Spirit makes it possible to experience God, rather than merely to think about him.

2. A *Lorica* deals with the world around you. There is no sense in recognizing the presence of trees, forests and lakes if you spend most of your time in an urban environment. Work into the prayer your present experience of life, including children, nature and man-made objects.

3. This type of prayer contains petitions asking God to protect you and your loved ones from harm. The words should be concrete, specific and brief. These petitions are not wish lists for something far in the future. They should deal with serious, immediate needs.

4. Your *Lorica* need not be long. Use the one in the story of St. Patrick as a model.

Second, memorize the "Christ be with me" part of St. Patrick's *Lorica*. It still has great value to those in need. Use it often.

When Christ
Is the Guest

There was a child who lived with his grandfather by the side of a busy road. One evening the grandfather and this child were outside listening to a meadowlark singing her clear, sweet song as she perched on the fence post. Suddenly they heard a commotion up the road. A crazy beggarman, with a tilt to his head and a glaze in his eye, was lurching up the lane. All the children of the town were chasing him, throwing sticks and stones. Even the dogs were nipping at his heels. As the beggarman passed the house, the grandfather could see the humiliation beneath a sheen of desperation on the man's face. The child, however, saw a chance to have some fun and joined in the teasing. He bent down, picked up a rock and ran to join his friends. Too old to move very fast, the grandfather could only call out to his grandson to come back. Above all the commotion, the meadowlark's song could be heard sweet and clear. The child broke from the group and ran back to his grandfather. Together they looked at the beggarman lurching and stumbling down the road chased by children and dogs.

The grandfather, eyes glistening with tears, knelt down and put his arms around the child. The child dropped the rock in his hand and touched the tear that rolled down his grandfa-

ther's cheek. "Grandpa," he said, "what's wrong?"

"Ah, laddie," said the grandfather, "would you be knowin' who that crazy beggarman was?"

"No, Grandpa," said the child.

"Well, I'm not sure as I know either, lad. But did you hear the lark? The lark was singing on the fence post, she was. And do you know what she was singing? There's words to her song, lad, and never forget them, for she was singing:

> *'Often, often, often, walks the Christ in the stranger's clothes.*
>
> *Often walks the Christ in the stranger's clothes.'"*

Two tears struck the ground, one shed from the face of the grandfather, the other from the eyes of the boy, as together they watched the King of Glory stumble down the road. Often walks the Christ in the stranger's clothes.

THE STRANGER

Do not neglect hospitality, for through it some have unknowingly entertained angels.

(Hebrews 13:1)

There are three ways to become truly aware of God in the everyday passage of life. The first of these is **hospitality**. Hospitality in this case does not mean good manners but rather the practice of charity in the real world. The quote from Scripture above refers to Abraham when he entertained three strangers only to find out later that they were the Lord and two angels. Hospitality was what enabled Abraham to become the father of nations, because God, as he was eating with Abraham, promised him and his wife, Sara, a son. Abraham's gift of hospitality was even greater than it appears, for he did this good thing without even knowing he was entertaining the Divine Presence.

In Christianity, particularly in the Celtic tradition, the stranger was respected, because one never knew if it might be Christ come visiting. The story above has, at its source, an ancient Celtic rune:

THE RUNE OF HOSPITALITY

I saw a stranger yesterevening,
I put food in the eating-place,
Drink in the drinking-place,
Music in the listening-place,
And in the Blessed Name of the Triune
He blessed myself and my house,
My cattle and my dear ones,
And the lark said in her song,
Often, often, often,
Walks the Christ in the stranger's guise,
Often, often, often,
Walks the Christ in the stranger's guise.[8]

It is impossible to overestimate the importance of hospitality. In ancient Ireland the poor were simply taken care of. The stranger was always welcomed. In modern times it is more difficult. We live in a culture of suspicion in which the stranger asking for a handout is treated with doubt and mistrust. As Christians, however, we are instructed to practice hospitality to the best of our ability, while taking into account modern needs for safety and caution.

The ancient Irish word for hospitality, *oigedchaire,* means "guest-loving." In the Christian vision of life the guest was always Christ.[9] An old Irish rhyme goes like this:

> *God in Heaven!*
> *The door of my house will always be*
> *Open to every traveler.*
> *May Christ open His to me!*
>
> *If you have a guest,*
> *And deny him anything in the house,*
> *It's not the guest you hurt.*
> *It's Christ you refuse.*[10]

The ancient Celts believed hospitality to the stranger was as good as a pilgrimage to Rome. Such importance was placed on hospitality that it had to be considered even when one was praying. John J. O'Riordain points out that for the ancient Celt "any form of inhospitable conduct is reprehensible, even in prayer. A prayer made for oneself alone is known in Irish as a *paidir ghann,* literally, a 'stingy prayer.'"[11]

Exactly how is this virtue of hospitality different from "being nice" or "being polite?" The answer lies in the openness of the human heart to Christ. At its essence, charity rests on the willingness of each man or woman to welcome Christ into his or her heart. The first person we must be hospitable to is Christ himself. Many people remember the popular folk painting of Christ at the door. It is a picture of a garden with Christ knocking at a doorway to get into a lovely cottage. Curiously, there is no latch on the door. It can only be opened from within. And that is precisely the point: Unless we admit the Lord of Love into our hearts, we will be unable to love another, much less the stranger.

The first step toward practicing hospitality to others is to be welcoming to the Lord. Several hundred years ago in Ireland, a tradition grew up of lighting a candle and placing it in a window on Christmas Eve. Legend had it that the Holy Family wandered the world at Christmas, looking for a place of welcome. The lighted candle would guide them to a welcoming home. But in the days when the Catholic faith was persecuted and priests were hunted down and killed throughout Ireland, the lighted candle at Christmas served not only to welcome the Holy Family but also to assure fugitive priests, outlawed by the British, that Midnight Mass could be celebrated safely for the people in that area. Anyone who was willing to leave their door open for the Lord could hardly refuse the need of one of his servants.

Hospitality is also different from social action. It has often seemed that many Christians now define their faith simply in how they help their fellow human beings. The practice of faith seems to have become a race to see how many food pantries can be opened, homeless shelters constructed, or little children clothed and fed. While helping others in need is part of the Christian mission, it is not necessarily hospitality. All too often our kindness to those less fortunate comes more from pity than love. We help because we feel sorry for them, not because we see them as Christ. The secular world we live in values Christians for our charitable impulses, but it does not understand why we do it. Even some Christians criticized Mother Teresa for her care of the poor. She was not seeking out the destruction of the things that caused poverty, they said. She was only picking drowning people out of a flooding river of woe instead of walking upriver and stopping the flood. They misunderstood Blessed Teresa, however. She wasn't practicing social action; she was practicing hospitality.

Pity is not a Christian virtue. Pity immediately lowers someone else and places us on a higher pedestal. Pity is condescending. Reaching down to assist those less fortunate may indeed help them, but it is often done out of selfish motivations, allowing us to maintain our own style of living. Hospitality immediately puts someone else in the place of Christ and makes us that person's servant. Acting hospitably comes out of wholly generous motivations. Honoring another human being made in the image of God ennobles the person practicing hospitality. Both people truly benefit.

Practically speaking, how does this virtue of hospitality work in real life? Obviously, we should not be foolish. We live in a culture of suspicion precisely because there are dangers from strangers. Problems arise, however, when we become paralyzed by our fear of what might happen and do nothing, instead of practicing hospitality in our daily lives. Running down to the worst parts of a major metropolitan city to help the nameless poor is a sure way to get into trouble. We are not experienced enough to handle those situations. But in Celtic Christianity, hospitality was practiced when someone came to your door, or when you met someone on a one-to-one basis in your daily activity. These are the simple encounters where this virtue is practiced and we become adept at it.

One of the great spiritual masters of the last century, Clarence Enzler, finishes his beautiful "Stations of the Cross" with Christ saying:

> *So seek me not in far-off places.*
> *I am close at hand.*
> *Your workbench, office, kitchen,*
> *these are altars*
> *where you offer love.*
> *And I am with you there.*[12]

Hospitality is a kindly virtue, a way of welcoming Christ and others. It can be practiced by anyone, anywhere. It is a hard virtue, however, for it consists of giving of ourselves without expecting return, of honoring others as if they were Jesus himself, and especially of realizing that we are no better than the people we are called to serve. All of us belong to the human condition; all of us are in solidarity with one another.

Meditation

Chapter twenty-five of Matthew's Gospel has been used by many spiritual masters as a meditative tool on how we treat others, how we will be perceived when we are judged, and how Christ settles the problem of evil and injustice in the world. We want to look at the Sermon on the Mount in terms of hospitality: not in how we have failed to act in a hospitable manner, but rather focusing on awareness of Christ's presence in those around us. Read the chapter out loud slowly and carefully. Don't analyze. Upon finishing, take out a notebook and after each phrase that Jesus utters ("When I was hungry, you gave me to eat..." "When I was thirsty you gave me to drink..."), write down the names of people who need your help. If you can't think of anyone you know, move on to the next phrase. Just do the people you know. There is no need to focus on our failings in hospitality yet. The reason for writing the names is to put faces on the commands of Christ. All of us know it is good to help those less fortunate, but if it happens to be an annoying coworker or a grouchy neighbor, our ideals are tempered by difficult personalities. Hospitality isn't easy. Writing down the specific names will demonstrate this. After finishing, spend a few moments thinking about these people and how you might find Christ in them.

Contemplation

Christ is knocking at the door of your heart. In a move from meditation (thinking about the image of Christ knocking on the door) to contemplation (simply resting in the presence of Christ), open the door of your heart to the Lord. Welcome him and let him in. This might be harder than it sounds. To welcome the Lord we have to be vulnerable and let go of our fears. If you have trouble doing this, move into contemplation by thinking of Christ emptying himself on the Cross out of love for you. Surrender yourself to Christ the same way.

Action

Make it a point to practice one or more of the corporal and spiritual works of mercy in the next twenty-four hours.

Corporal Works of Mercy

Feed the hungry
Give drink to the thirsty
Clothe the naked
Shelter the homeless
Visit the sick
Visit the imprisoned
Bury the dead

Spiritual Works of Mercy

Counsel the doubtful
Instruct the ignorant
Admonish the sinner
Comfort the sorrowful
Forgive injuries
Bear wrongs patiently
Pray for the living
and the dead

Christ in the Ordinary

There was a woman who lived in a small house in the countryside with her family. Upon rising each morning she would splash her face with water three times in the name of the Holy Trinity, saying:

The palmful of the God of Life,
The palmful of the Christ of Love
The palmful of the Spirit of Peace,
Triune of grace.

She would watch her husband and her son go out with the men of the village to fish each morning. They would sing:

The day of light has come upon us,
Christ is born of the Virgin.

In His name I sprinkle the water
Upon everything within my court.

Thou King of deeds and powers above,
Thy fishing blessing pour down on us.

I will sit me down with an oar in my grasp,
I will row me seven hundred and seven strokes.

I will cast down my hook,
The first fish which I bring up.

In the name of Christ, King of the elements,
The poor shall have it at his wish.

And the king of fishers, the brave Peter,
He will after it give me his blessing.

Ariel, Gabriel and John,
Raphael benign, and Paul,

Columba, tender in every distress,
And Mary fair, the endowed of grace,

Encompass ye us to the fishing-bank of ocean,
And still ye to us the crest of the waves.

Be the King of kings at the end of our course,
Of lengthened life and of lasting happiness.

Be the crown of the King from the Three on high,
Be the cross of Christ adown to shield us,

The crown of the King from the Three on high,
The cross of Christ adown to shield us.

And she would return to her duties, praying an invocation to the Trinity and reflecting on life itself.

> *I make this bed*
> *In the name of the Father, the Son and the Holy*
>   *Ghost,*
> *In the name of the night that we were conceived,*
> *In the name of the night that we were born,*
> *In the name of the day that we were baptized,*
> *In the name of each night, each day,*
> *Each angel that is in the heavens.*

And when the day was done, her husband and son sent off to bed, she would sit down by the fire in the kitchen and begin to smoor or bank the fire so that the embers would burn low in the night to be refreshed again by her in the morning. The blocks of peat had to be arranged just so, the embers evenly spread on the hearth in the shape of a circle. Dividing the circle into three in honor of the Trinity, she would lay a block of peat in each of the sections, the first in the name of the God of Life, the second in the name of the God of Peace, the third in the name of the God of Grace: three persons, one God; three peats, one flame. When finished, she would stretch forth her hand in blessing and say:

> *I am smooring the fire*
> *As the Son of Mary would smoor;*
> *Blest be the house, blest be the fire,*
>   *Blest be the people all.*

Who are those down on the floor?
John and Peter and Paul.
On whom is this vigil tonight?
On the fair gentle Mary and on her Son.

The mouth of God said,
The angel of God spake,
An angel in the door of the house,
To guard and to keep us all
Till daylight tomorrow.

Oh! may the angels of the Holy One of God
Environ me all this night,
Oh! may the angels of the Anointed One of God
Encompass me from harm and from evil,
Oh! encompass me from harm this night.

First to rise, last to sleep, she would leave the embers burning, her house protected by Christ, his Mother, the angels and the saints. The family would rest, asleep in the arms of the Lord.[13]

If you are aware of the proximity of the heavenly world, then you become aware of the holiness of the everyday. All actions done in love, caring or generosity can lead a person to God, even the humblest, like a woman smooring or banking the evening fire before bed.

No doubt those pastoral images in the meditation above speak clearly of another time, another place, when life was a bit slower and people lived closer to the land. But truth is always the same, and what these peasant people discovered without their college degrees and six-figure salaries was a pearl of great price, a treasure in the field. To know that each action during the day has great spiritual significance transforms each day into an opportunity to discover a bit more about God, love a little more deeply, and realize that even in the most mundane of tasks the presence of the Trinity can be felt.

Making work holy is the virtue at issue here. The Christian faith has used many images and examples to keep this virtue foremost in the minds of people throughout the years. The charming example of Joseph teaching the Christ Child how to saw, hammer and mold wood in his carpenter shop is an image that still brings home to us the knowledge that Jesus grew up in the house of a working family, one bound together by religion and faith. Indeed, the example of the Holy Family reminds people of the simple values of family living and the importance of working together. In times past, the family itself was able to unite the work, play and rest its members experienced into a cohesive whole, a routine and comforting pattern of life. In Catholic homes throughout the past two centuries it was quite common for the day to end in prayer with a family rosary in the dining or living room. God was simply part of the everyday. This was no mystical experience, at least not usually. Instead it was part of life, an awareness that God infused our human experiences with his presence.

Nowadays, however, it seems we can hardly draw a breath of peace and relaxation throughout our day. In the dawn of the twenty-first century our modern lives are frenetic, stressful, characterized by the "24-7" culture in which we live. Each day begins after a night of insufficient sleep, and exhaustion dogs our steps as we seek to make more money, advance in our career, amass more possessions. We are not consciously greedy, but like the rich fool in one of Jesus' parables who sees his worldly advances causing him stress and frustration, we forget the meaning of life. God speaks to him, saying, " 'You fool! This very night your life is being demanded of you. And the things you have prepared, whose will they be?' So it is with those who store up treasure for themselves but are not rich toward God" (Luke 12:20-21).

Even our children learn to adopt this attitude. We push them hard to excel, to win, to achieve. We yell at the umpires at little league games, we place our own unfulfilled childhood upon the backs of our sons and daughters, urging them to use the opportunities we've given them to succeed where we once failed. Our children learn the empty pursuit of ambition: If they are not number one at something, they quickly abandon what they enjoy to find something else in which they can be more successful. Mother Teresa, however, once said, "God has not called me to be successful, but to be faithful." Without the recognition of work as holy labor dedicated to the Creator, we get lost in the rat race of our society.

Upon retirement, many people often feel a sense of emptiness and loss. With the drive for success no longer relevant, they wonder at the value of what they spent their lives doing. But what ennobles our lives is not which particular job we did or how successful we were at it, but how we did it and for whom. Our work is our acknowledgment that God made us in his image and that when we work we give glory to God. We praise him for the gifts he has given. By consecrating our work to God, we remind ourselves of the holiness of labor, and our work in fact becomes our prayer, another way for us to commune with God. That realization can bring new meaning to the most mundane of jobs, ennobling us in the process.

In Catholic schools in the 1940's, 50's, and 60's, religious sisters taught millions of students to honor their work. Though it is doubtful that a cross and the letters "AMDG" (Latin abbreviation for the phrase "All for the honor and glory of God") meant an immediate realization of the value of work to a sixth grader initialing them at the top of a math assignment, it serves as an example for us today. That simple gesture on homework papers—and extended metaphorically to the rest of our lives—represents the Church's effort to emphasize the holiness of work.

So what should we do today? Sign our tax return with the sign of the cross? Bless the work we do on a factory line with holy water? Before deciding on an action we should focus on the attitude. For instance, how many of us pray a blessing upon our food when we go out to eat? Seldom is the sign of the cross made at the nearest fast food place we stumble into at the end of a long day or during a rushed noon hour. We are embarrassed to display our faith in public, so rather than make holy a very natural part of our day, we do nothing, lest we draw attention to ourselves and risk puzzled stares or ridicule. In other words, we are confused about what we should do, because we are more worried about embarrassment than we are about recognizing that God has chosen the dignity of the ordinariness of the everyday to reveal his presence.

Once we realize that God gives us ordinary tasks and moments during the day to get to know him better and grow in holiness and charity towards others, we will begin to do things that reflect that new attitude: praying on our way to work; taking a few moments during a break to speak to God about how the day is going; asking God to bless a particularly difficult interview, meeting or task we must attend to today. All these are simple things to bind us ever more closely to the one who made us.

Many of us work in jobs we do not like, with people with whom we would not otherwise associate, who talk about values and experiences we do not share. In a pluralistic society, like the one we live in, we shrink from opportunities to share our faith, worried as we are about being accused of proselytizing. Finding ways to be joyful about our faith—and to explain what and why we believe what we believe—is surely one of the best ways to make holy our work.

Wherever God is, there is life. Our recognition that God is with us during the day will energize our work and make us more productive. Knowing that God is by our side will help us work better, be less distracted by other workers who disturb us, and make us more creative. Why? Because we will not simply be working for money or advancement, we will be praying our work by doing it for God.

Sound too simplistic? Remember the experience of the monks. As the Church began to spread throughout the world, people seeking God started monasteries and hermitages. Always, along with prayer, work was one of the central components of monastic life. *Ora et Labora* (Work and Pray) was St. Benedict's motto, and he was the founder of western monasticism. We may not be monks, but we have to recognize that the elevation of labor to a necessary component on the path to holiness means we cannot ignore the obvious: Work dedicated to God makes us closer to the Lord. If a Celtic peasant, like the woman mentioned in the opening story of this chapter, illiterate and stuck on the Hebridean Islands off the coast of Scotland, could figure this out one hundred and fifty years ago, surely we in our supposedly sophisticated culture can do the same.

Meditation

In the Sermon on the Mount (Matthew 5-7), Jesus spends a great deal of time on how to set our priorities. Statements like, "Do not store up for yourselves treasures on earth...but store up for yourselves treasures in heaven....For where your treasure is, there also will your heart be," talk about the need to let the worldly worries go and embrace the things of God. Read the famous passage below and apply it to your life. What about your daily existence causes you anxiety and worry? Is it possible to do your daily duties for the glory of God rather than out of a need to amass possessions or power? Is there room for trust in your life? How can you bless the cares of the day and make them opportunities to praise God?

[Jesus said,]"Therefore I tell you, do not worry about your life, what you will eat or what you will drink, or about your body, what you will wear. Is not life more than food, and the body more than clothing? Look at the birds of the air; they neither sow nor reap nor gather into barns, and yet your heavenly Father feeds them. Are you not of more value than they? And can any of you by worrying add a single hour to your span of life? And why do you worry about clothing? Consider the lilies of the field, how they grow; they neither toil nor spin, yet I tell you, even Solomon in all his glory was not clothed like one of these. But if God so clothes the grass of the field, which is alive today and tomorrow is thrown into the oven, will he not much more clothe you—you of little faith? Therefore do not worry, saying 'What will we drink?' or 'What will we wear?' For it is the Gentiles who strive for all these things; and indeed your heavenly Father knows that you need all these things. But strive first for the kingdom of God and his righteousness, and all these things will be given to you as well. So do not worry about tomorrow, for tomorrow will bring worries of its own. Today's trouble is enough for today." (Matthew 6:25-34)

Contemplation

In a quiet place, at a quiet time, allow God to encompass you. No words now but these: "Lord, I trust in you." Repeat them every time you sense a distracting thought coming into your mind. Set a timer if you must, but spend at least fifteen minutes doing this and allow the powerful presence of the Lord to envelop you. He is there to protect and sustain you.

Action

Write down three ways you can make your work holy, ways you can become aware of the presence of God in your daily activity, and then try them this week. It's not enough just to say, "I will consciously call to mind God's presence." These three ways have to be actions, not mental constructs. For example, you can bless your work with the Sign of the Cross, bless your desk with a crucifix, or affix the cross on the paper you are working, even if it is simply tracing the cross on your work with your hand or finger. These are the types of actions that concretely call to mind that you are dedicating your work to God.

In the Shadow
of the Cross

*Therefore, since we are surrounded by so great a cloud of
witnesses, let us also lay aside every weight and the sin
that clings so closely, and let us run with perseverance the
race that is set before us, looking to Jesus the pioneer and
perfecter of our faith, who for the sake of the joy that was
set before him endured the cross, disregarding its shame,
and has taken his seat at the right hand of the throne of
God.*

(Hebrews 12:1-2)

*Twelve hundred years ago no cities dotted the Irish landscape.
Instead the people clustered around huge monasteries which
were the centers of Irish civilization. Monasteries of men and
women had existed for centuries, and lay folk blended in with
the community, setting up the necessities for life around the
monastery perimeter. The monastic system had merged well
with the Irish tribal culture in which a whole village was considered extended family. Schools flourished, artisans excelled
in gold and silver work, and illuminated manuscripts soared
to heights never seen anywhere else in the world. While Europe
fell into the night of the Dark Ages, the light of learning and*

culture burned brightly in this tiny corner of humanity...until the dragon ships came.

It was about this time, when the great monasteries were at their height, that the silent ships of the Vikings, long and lean, came sailing up the Shannon River. As the boats slipped like knives through the water, a horrific cry would erupt from the decks as pagan Norsemen ran up the banks towards the monastery to plunder and pillage, to rape and kill. For over one hundred years this happened with frightening regularity, and the spiritual and artistic treasures of the monasteries were destroyed, learning was interrupted, and civilization teetered on the brink of extinction. Monks and nuns, women and children, innocent people all, felt the bite of the sword ending their life. The faith of the people seemed lost, and then the creativity of the Irish was fully revealed.

They began to carve in stone the record of their lives of faith. Shortly before the invasions distinctive stone crosses with their characteristic circle around the center of the cross began to appear. Simple at first, they swiftly grew in complexity and size once the Vikings came. The Great High Crosses of Ireland stood up to thirteen feet high. Devoid of monetary value, they were left alone by the Vikings. But on the base and arms of the crosses the Irish sculpted pictures from the Scriptures that illustrated the importance and meaning of the Cross of Christ and sustained them throughout the terrible times caused by the pagan Norsemen. The Sacrifice of Isaac; the Three Young Men in the Fiery Furnace; Adam and Eve; events from the Life, Passion and Death of Christ; St. Michael carrying out Christ's Judgment; the Coming of Christ at the End of Time: all these were *favorite bas reliefs on the High Crosses.*

These crosses were created to show the everlasting nature of the faith that even the cruel Vikings could not destroy. The books of the Irish may have been burned or stolen, the gold and silver chalices and cups melted down, but the faith of the people simply found a new way to express itself. Around these stone crosses with their pictures of salvation and judgment, the children would gather and be taught the stories of faith. In the centuries to come, as the Irish knew persecution from other foreign invaders, these crosses were used as teaching tools and symbols of hope. Many of them still stand today, for they represent the rock of faith that cannot be destroyed—Jesus Christ.

or all Christians the Cross of Christ is at the center of their faith. Particularly for Catholic Christians, a cross or crucifix is a common sight in homes. We recognize, at least subconsciously, that our lives are forever changed by that piece of wood and the body that hangs on it. The same motivation that drove the Irish to create the High Crosses, namely to discover the mystery and meaning of Jesus Christ, moves inside us, though we often do not acknowledge it. Herein lies our problem: Without really understanding the Cross, our faith will have no meaning. Without recognizing its power, we will not see it as the defining feature of our lives. Without standing in the shadow of its majesty, we will remain distant to the God who sent his Son to save us.

When we recall the power of the Cross, when we as Christians allow the Cross to be the most important symbol of our lives, then the message to the Hebrews that began this chapter makes sense. Our lives have a goal in which we are unfortunately handicapped, but we have the inspiration of those who have gone before us and the example of Christ to lead us on.[14]

The Cross reminds us that we have a goal: We are running a race in this life towards God, towards good, towards the light. We don't just exist in this world simply to be alive. We have a destiny. The Cross is the goal of the Christian, for it represents the final defeat of sin, the triumph of goodness, and the reward of eternal life. It is what we see on the horizon of our life—our road of sorrow, our way of joy. It is a symbol that stands both for joy and sorrow. For Christians, the Cross is what gives meaning to life. Most of us probably wouldn't or couldn't say it that way, but we know that God means for us to be saved and that to be saved we must respond to Christ's invitation to follow him all the way to Calvary and beyond.

The Cross reminds us that we are sinners. It was our sins that Jesus died for. Many people recoil in shock at this notion that we are responsible for the death of Christ. Thinking that the Church wants to make us feel guilty, we often get very angry about admitting our sinfulness.

We are handicapped by our faults and failings, our sins, and we need to clearly see this. The Cross stands for the virtues of *salvation* and *judgment*. In a time when everyone wants to hear about niceness and blame all wrongdoing on dysfunctional families or addictions or chemical imbalances, the Cross is a piercing light of truth for our day and age. It is the corrective.

The Celtic Christians knew the story of the Cross. Christ did not just die on the Cross because he was the victim of a few bad men. He died for us, because of our sins. This is a crucial point, because if we did not put Christ on the Cross, if we are guilty of no sin, then what do we need Jesus for? Most Christians acknowledge that Jesus was a good man, a teacher, someone we should look up to, but many have forgotten that his primary importance is that of Savior, Redeemer, Lord and God.

When we stand in the shadow of the Cross, we are judged. Christ died for the sins of all. Anything evil we have done is part of the sinfulness for which Christ died. To the believer, the judgment at the foot of the Cross is not guilt-producing. It is an experience of mercy and salvation. For the one who believes in what Jesus did, there is no other judgment than that of mercy.

This puts the whole idea of heaven and hell in a new light. On the High Crosses of Ireland we find many pictures of salvation, such as the Resurrection, Jesus' appearance to the three Marys, the saving of the men in the fiery furnace, and so on. But we also find scenes of damnation, St. Michael weighing souls in the balance, angels blowing trumpets, devils leading souls to hell. In our modern age we do not like to think that God will ever condemn us. One of the great Celtic writers, Daphne Pouchin Mould says,

We have forgotten what justice and mercy stand for. To us, the two concepts stand opposed: We think of mercy as softness, even as letting a man alone to go his own way, whilst justice to us still appears armed with a sword....We like, for our own comfort, to imagine Him merely as merciful; merciful in the sense that He will let us alone to please ourselves and then overlook all we have done. But that would contradict justice and contradict the teaching of the Cross....St. Augustine was well aware of this feeling that God will damn nobody. He saw it as another variant of the devil's wiles in Eden....But the evidence for eternal happiness is the same as that for eternal damnation: You cannot believe Christ when he promises heaven and disbelieve him when he threatens hell. If we doubt the eternity of damnation, we must also doubt the eternity of blessedness.[15]

For the true believer, however, fear of hell is not the motivating factor in faith. Rather, it is the realization that it was for our sins that Christ died. He died so that we might live. That fear of the Last Judgment is not for the faithful, but only for those who have denied the relevance of God.

For those of us who believe, the Cross is our inspiration. Looking at the High Crosses of Ireland one sees that love and mercy stand out most clearly. Why? Because the Cross is for believers, and though it reminds us why Jesus had to come, it also reminds us that he came as one of us. The Virgin Mary bore him, taught him to walk and talk. He suffered hunger and fear, he knew sickness and loneliness, he was one of us. That's why it is important that we hold on to the themes of salvation and judgment. Yes, we can be damned, but that is not the will of the Father. He will do everything to save us. Only our stubbornness and rejection will condemn us. The Cross remains a beacon of hope in a world of violence and sin, and the one who pays attention to that beacon is saved, saved by the God who walked among us as one of us. It is the Cross that gives meaning to history and to each of our lives. As St. Francis taught us to say, "We adore you, O Christ, and we praise you, because by your Holy Cross you have redeemed the world!"

We ought to take inspiration from the cloud of witnesses that surrounds us—the saints who have already borne witness to the Lord by their lives. They have completed their struggle and journey, and like an audience watching the Olympic races they are there cheering us on as we run our own race in life. But because they have already gone through what we are going through, they inspire us even more. As the Scripture scholar William Barclay says, "An athlete would strive with double effort if he knew that a stadium of famous Olympic athletes was watching him. It is of the very essence of Christian life that it is lived in the gaze of the heroes of the faith who lived, suffered and died in their day and generation. How can anyone avoid the struggle for greatness with an audience like that looking down upon him?"[16]

Of course we have the example of Christ to guide us. After all, Christ was spit upon, beaten, reviled and cursed by the world of his day. The world thought he was foolish and his values ridiculous. People laughed at his concept of life, and yet with the Cross comes a crown. The circle that goes around the Celtic Cross tells it most clearly: Those who are despised by the world for the sake of Christ ultimately conquer the world.

The Sign of the Cross was an automatic gesture for the Celtic Christians. They blessed everything and often. Quoting Tertullian, O'Riordain says: "At every step, at every movement, when we go in or out, when we dress or put on our shoes, at the bath, at table, when lights are brought, when we retire to bed, when we sit down, whatever we do, we mark our foreheads with the sign of the Cross."[17] They could have just thought about the Cross, but instead it was important for them to sign all important people and things with this great symbol. When we enter a church we make this sign and we do so at the beginning of prayer. Not an empty gesture, the Sign of the Cross remains the major way we identify ourselves as Christians, redeemed by the Lord, recipients of his loving mercy.

Meditation

Find a spot to pray for about fifteen minutes and picture the Crucifixion. There is Christ, on the hill of Calvary. At the foot of the Cross is his mother, Mary, and his best friend, John. All other friends and family have fled. Into this scene you step. You approach the foot of the Cross. You touch the shoulder of John, the hand of the Blessed Virgin Mary. Then you look up and gaze at the suffering face of Christ. He opens his eyes and looks down upon you. What do you say to him? What is it that you most wish to communicate to him? Speak those words now. How does he respond? What does he say to you?

Contemplation

After finishng your meditation, sit with a crucifix and focus on Christ. Whenever you feel distracted, simply pray the prayer St. Francis gave us, "We adore you, O Christ, and we praise you, because by your holy Cross you have redeemed the world." Spend significant time (ten to fifteen minutes) and then close with an Our Father.

Action

If your home does not have a crucifix, get one. A crucifix is different than a cross; a crucifix has the image of Christ hanging on it. This is important, because by itself the Cross means nothing. It is what Jesus did on it that matters. Next, begin to bless those things that have significance to you. You probably think that only priests or deacons can bless. Not true! Anyone may ask God's blessing on another person. The prayer is as simple as you wish. Just ask God's blessing and add the relevant details. Perhaps the best way to do this is to start with your loved ones, particularly spouse and children. To bless a loved one before sleep, to entrust the little ones to the care of Christ, to trace that sign on the foreheads of the people we care for, all that is a powerful symbol of the encompassing presence of God. Besides, kids love it and will ask for it. It will become a routine and welcome part of family prayer.

The Celtic Virtue of Repentance

The Cross of Christ

Saint Columba was a man who loved books. Hand-made, beautifully illuminated, written on vellum (a material made from the hide of a sheep or cow) and painted in beautiful colors, the books of his age were artistic treasures to behold. Columba himself produced many of them. Skilled he was as a scribe, and he was always on the lookout for a beautiful manuscript.

Columba was a prince and could even have been High King of all Ireland had he not accepted God's call. By the time he was forty he was the most famous of all churchmen in the land, having started many monasteries. Passionate, eloquent, strong and good looking, Columba gave his religious vocation stature and respect throughout the land. Kings and wise men listened to him.

One day, not so long after his fortieth birthday, Columba chanced to visit the monastery of an old friend who was abbot there. The abbot showed Columba a treasure he had returned with from Rome: a beautifully illuminated psalter. Columba gasped at its beauty, and his good heart grew dark. He wanted it badly. He could not steal it from his friend, but he could copy it. In the wee hours of the night, for many nights running, he crept from his bed and went to the library where he copied and copied until he had produced a perfect copy of the abbot's book. He was just finishing the last word when the abbot chanced to walk into the library. "What have you done?" said the abbot in horror. "You were my friend, and yet you have crept into my library and copied my treasure! Give the copy to me and get out of my sight you faithless, duplicitous man!" And Columba did leave, but he took his copy with him.

The abbot went to the High King and demanded justice. At the trial Columba was forced to stand before the King and hear the judgment given. The King decreed that Columba had, in effect, stolen the abbot's book. The King then uttered the famous lines, "To every cow her calf; to every book its copy." Columba, however, refused to give the book back. His pride got the better of him, "I am a prince," he said, "and I and my family defy you. We do not recognize the jurisdiction of this court. We will go to war rather than give up this book."

And so began the darkest days of Columba's life. In his rage and anger he heated up the passions of his tribe and inflamed them to wage war. The armies of Columba's family and the armies of the High King met in the shadow of Benbulben on the plains of Cul Drummin. On a high rock above the fray stood Columba in robes of gray. His arms held aloft, like Moses of old, he prayed to God for victory. And as the sun shone down on the purple heather, the blood ran red in the fields. The forces of Columba's family destroyed the armies of the High King, and Columba exulted in victory. Beneath him lay the bodies of 3,000 dead, and he exulted, until he saw other gray robes walking amidst the battlefield, blessing the dead, tending the wounded. They were monks from a monastery nearby that he himself had founded. "What have I done?" he cried in horror. Appalled by the events he set in motion, he went down to join his monks on the fields of the dead.

Columba had to answer for what he did. At a church assembly, the facts were laid out. It was clear what happened, but there were extenuating circumstances. Columba's family had been seeking for a way to diminish the High King's power, and the Battle of the Book proved to be a good excuse. Even the abbot, Columba's friend, was remorseful. "Had I not been so angry, I would not have provoked my dear Columba," he said. But Columba would have none of it. He knew he was wrong, that his pride and greed had caused the deaths of thousands. He resolved to leave Ireland and sail for the first island where he could no longer see the Emerald Isle. And that is how he came to Iona of Scotland and how he redeemed himself for the evil he had caused as he brought the light of the Gospel to a land which knew not Christ. He asked for forgiveness from God whom he had offended and from the people he had harmed. Not one to dwell on the past, he trusted in the mercy of God and turned this sorrow into joy. For his exile proved a blessing, and from his repentance the land of Scotland turned to Christ.[18]

SAINT AND SINNER

he Cross is a sign of salvation and judgment but it is also an instrument that moves us to action. It gives to us the moral aspect of our life. The Cross brings us squarely to our actions in this world as Christians. As Pope John Paul II said in his encyclical, *Veritatis Splendor (The Splendor of Truth),* "Faith is not merely an intellectual assent to certain abstract truths; it also possesses a moral content."[19] This means that belief requires action. Even Jesus tells us, "Not everyone who says to me 'Lord, Lord' will enter the kingdom of heaven, but only the one who does the will of my Father who is in heaven" (Matthew 7:21).

In many respects, truth in our modern society has become fuzzied, blurred by our unwillingness to face it. Truth is not relative. Truth, morality, good and evil all have become constructs within our own minds and subject to whatever faults and weaknesses we might have. It is easy to justify adultery if we mask it with words of love. It is easy to justify the oppression of the poor if we insist on the survival of the fittest. It is easy to justify just about anything when our own personal happiness becomes the criteria on which we judge the rightness or wrongness of any action. The Cross, however, reminds us of where humanity has come—from sin—and where humanity is going—to glory—and we cannot get there without Christ. We have to go through the Cross to get there. There are certain things that are always right and always wrong.

St. Paul said it well when he wrote, "The Cross of Christ [must] not be emptied of its power" (1 Corinthians 1:17). To stand at the foot of the Cross is not some sentimental exercise, but rather it must lead to concrete action. There is no break between faith and morality. A person cannot believe one thing and act differently in public. Being Christian means acting like Christ wants us to, not as we wish. Membership in the Church, says the Pope, is not decided on the basis of faith alone. Our actions carry just as much weight, if not more.[20]

The corruption of this view, even by members of our own faith, is easy to see. Politicians are often the unfortunate scapegoats of our society, but the very nature of their public lives make them an easy example for all to see. Often a politician might say, "I personally believe this, but I cannot foist my personal beliefs on other people." That might be fine on minor issues, but on grander issues of right and wrong our faith demands action. If the truth is out there rather than just in me, then I have an obligation to help others see the truth and encourage public policy along those lines. Issues of life and death have right or wrong answers. To say this may appear that we are binding ourselves in chains, but to be shackled to the truth is true freedom.

This is a hard message for many to hear. We think that freedom means doing anything we want, but the Christian concept of freedom means following the Cross, for *it* is the truth that sets us free. And if God is real Truth, then the more we follow his commands, the more truly alive we can be. Freedom isn't doing what we want. It's following God's Truth.

Since the events of September 11, 2001, people throughout the world have experienced a difficult dose of reality. Evil isn't just an abstract concept anymore. The actions that snuffed out the lives of thousands had to be labeled. Old concepts of good and evil were resurrected and many people discovered for the first time that evil really does exist.

Many Catholics have severe disagreements with the Church in a variety of areas, particularly sexuality and reproductive issues, but the Church cannot simply change these essential moral teachings. Other moral transgressions may be more common, but that does not make them acceptable. Adultery is always going to be wrong. Pedophilia is always going to be wrong. Greed is always going to be wrong. When we fail, as we occasionally will, then we look for the forgiveness that the Cross of Christ gives to those who seek to follow the Lord. To be truly free we have no choice but to do as Jesus says: "If anyone wishes to come after me, he must deny himself and take up his cross daily and follow me." (Luke 9:23) The Church has always been pretty black and white in her precepts but very compassionate in her application of them to real life.

In a world where people hate to admit their sinfulness, we can all learn a lesson from Columba. He teaches us the virtue of *repentance*. He sinned seriously, but he did not make excuses for his actions. He repented and got on with his life. He knew that falling down was bad enough, but refusing to get back up was even worse. He was not a prisoner to guilt. Unfortunately, failure to get back up is an option many people choose in their spiritual lives. They sin so often they forget what they are doing and become comfortable living in the slums of life, just like the prodigal son. That young man thought he was having the time of his life—booze, sex, money—and then one day he woke up in the dirt with the pigs and realized he had sinned. He came to his senses. He forced himself to admit that he had sinned, and once he did that his repentance was assured. He rushed right out and found his father and was forgiven.

In both the examples of St. Columba and the prodigal son, action followed repentance. Once they knew that they were sorry, they went to confess their sin. Many of us have no problem shooting a quick "I'm sorry" up to that distant God in the heavens, but we have a very difficult time confessing those sins to a priest, who represents both God and the people we have offended. Most people reading this book will not have been to the Sacrament of Penance for quite some time. Unsure of its efficacy or necessity, many procrastinate and thus perpetuate the myth that this particular sacrament is not for them. "Why confess my sins to a priest?" they ask. "I already told God I was sorry."

The Sacrament of Reconciliation (also called the Sacrament of Penance) can be a liberating experience. Think of a young child and his mother after the child has done something very wrong. The child knows that ultimately his mother will forgive him, but he still feels the need to go to his mother and apologize. He wants to feel her arm around him as she says, "It's okay. I forgive you. Just don't do it again." The child is then on his best behavior, at least temporarily, helping out with chores and being good. So it is with confession. It is a ritual in which the words of forgiveness, which come from God, are spoken to us and we feel God's forgiving touch. We need to actually say out loud what we did wrong, announce that we are sorry, and then do something to demonstrate our willingness to sin no more. Intellectually, we know that God will forgive us, but in order to really experience that forgiveness, we need to do penance.

The Sacrament of Penance is the ritual way we apologize to God and God speaks words of forgiveness to us. Is it the only way to be forgiven? No. But it is the Catholic way, and the Catholic way is the human way. What child would presume the forgiveness of mom? Why should we presume the forgiveness of God? We need to be an active participant in this celebration of forgiveness, or else we are not in personal relationship with God.

Meditation

Again, picture yourself standing at the foot of the Cross. This time, with pen and paper in hand, jot down the conflict areas of your life. In other words, write down the moral conflicts you have with God, with the Church, with others. Then note how you deal with these conflicts when you speak about these issues with others. For instance, if you are conflicted over premarital sex, what do you tell young people? Or if you think it is okay to cheat on your taxes, how do you explain that to your son or daughter? After doing this, speak directly to Christ about these issues as you look up at him on the Cross. Can you sustain your view in front of our Lord? What does he say to you about these issues? Is it consistent with what you find him saying in the Scriptures and in the tradition of our faith?

Contemplation

This part only works if you believe there are moral absolutes, that God has placed a truth in our hearts that is above our own wishes and desires and thoughts. Again at the foot of the Cross, as its shadow falls on you, offer up your conflicts and confusions and simply be with the crucified Christ. As you rest in quiet with him, if you have any mental distractions, simply use the phrase, "The truth shall set me free," to return to the foot of the Cross.

Action

First, pick one of the moral questions that most vexes you and take time to understand the Church's teaching on that issue. One of the things Catholicism values is intellectual honesty. There are reasons for believing what we believe. Investigate and see if new information changes your views.

Second, go to the Sacrament of Penance. Did you know that the Celtic monks from Ireland were the ones who pushed the idea of frequent individual private confession of sins? It comes from their belief that everyone should have an *anamchara*—a soul friend. They believed, and convinced the rest of the Church, that this way of celebrating the Sacrament of Penance was not only a fine way to receive forgiveness but also a great way to receive grace—a strengthening of heart, mind and soul. If it has been a while since you last went to confession, be at peace. Simply tell the priest how long it has been, and he will help you. Don't pick an unknown priest unless absolutely necessary. Go to one whom you trust and with whom you have had some experience. Then make it a habit to experience this sacrament regularly. It is not just about forgiveness. It is also about receiving the grace to not sin again.

The Celtic Virtue of Asceticism

Spiritual Aerobics

On the shores of Clew Bay, in the west of Ireland, rises a grey mountain, lonely and forbidding. It has always been a holy place. Two thousand five hundred feet above the shoreline it towers alone, cone-shaped and dark. The Druids had a shrine there, until St. Patrick came and spent an extraordinary Lent on that sacred mountain. It is called Croagh Patrick—the holy mountain of St. Patrick. Forty days and forty nights he battled demons. Like black crows they were, attacking him mercilessly. He went there to wrestle with the devil and win a land for Christ. They say he drove the snakes from there, and like Abraham he argued with God to save a people, this time the Irish. But as he came down the mountain, an angel sent to him white birds of Paradise to cheer him on and light his way.

Pilgrims come throughout the year, but none so many as on the last Sunday of July, when tens of thousands make the hour and a half ascent to the top. Old people and young, single or with families, they climb. Some walk barefoot. And as they pass the statue of St. Patrick at the base of the mountain they step away from this time and place into a holy space. Even the ever-present fog and mist sweeps upward, beckoning the climber to ascend. Why do they climb?

There is no other holy mountain like it. It is majestic, but dark and brooding, a place of conflict. People climb to confront the darkness of their lives, their own personal demons. The last few hundred yards are the hardest for the pilgrim. The effort is great, the will falters, but there is a gift for the pilgrim at the summit. If one is blessed, the mist clears and the sun shines bright on Clew Bay, half a mile below with its hundreds of green islands in the blue shining water. Even the great British author William Thackeray wrote that the beauty of that sight was not to be equaled on earth. For the pilgrim the climb is worth it, because after struggle comes clarity and beauty. But it usually is just a brief glimpse until the clouds and mist descend again. The path downward is one of relief, with the inscrutable mountain whispering in the mists, "Renew the struggle; do not give up; embrace the pain, the light, the shadow; go back into the world." Does one meet God on the mountain? It is a holy mountain, but unlike the awesomeness of Mt. Sinai, where the thunder of Yahweh still echoes, or the beauty of Mt. Krizevac in Medjugorje, where the Blessed Mother is still said to speak, God communicates more obliquely and quietly at Croagh Patrick, like the still, small voice Elijah heard on Mt. Carmel. After the effort, the pain, and the conflict are endured, the heart of the pilgrim—like the summit of the mountain—clears and for a moment he or she glimpses a vision of what paradise looks like and hears the actual presence of God walking in the evening breeze. God is there on Croagh Patrick, and every true pilgrim leaves with a cheered heart, seeing visions of the same white birds of Paradise that Patrick saw on his descent.

ne of the great scenes in film history is the beginning of *The Sound of Music.* The camera pans across the Austrian Alps, tall and forbidding. Then it begins to zero in on one mountain, and we come close to the jagged peaks. Suddenly, a plateau full of green grass and flowers appears, and in the middle of the green field, surrounded by the tops of mountains, is a young nun, swirling around in the midst of beauty and singing, "The hills are alive with the sound of music!" No doubt about it, that scene takes your breath away. But none of us ask the obvious question: How did she get up there? As beautiful and spectacular as that sight is, it must have taken her a lot of effort to reach such a place where she felt so truly alive. To touch the heavens, she had to climb the jagged rocks. Would any of us make such an effort?

In this new millennium, many of us fall prey to the latest weight-loss gimmick, the newest exercise machine. Our basements and attics are littered with gizmos that give us everything we needed to lose weight—except, of course, the will necessary to accomplish that goal. And yet we try and try to stay in shape. Often it is a losing battle; witness the rise of obesity in our culture. Yet we see the need to try to keep our bodies in shape in order that we might stay physically healthy. It is curious, however, that most of us pay no attention to the fact that our souls also need a good workout—frequently and regularly—to stay in shape. "Spiritual aerobics" is just as necessary as physical exercise if we are truly going to be wholly healthy. Climb an earthly mountain and you get to see the beauty of the world. Ascend a spiritual mountain and you just might get to see the face of God.

Asceticism is spiritual aerobics. It is the virtue that will help us carry the Cross of Christ. Daphne Mould tells us that when looking at the Celts' love of nature and the high hills of Ireland we must realize:

> [There is] a price to be paid for the freedom of the hills, the ascent has a penitential side to it. There is a renunciation of the comfortable things of this world, the snugness of the glen and the fireside, the shelter of the wood and the ease of smooth walking, for the rock and the sting of wind-driven hail—and the splendor of the beauty of the summits. It is the paradox of Christianity that you must, as it were, abandon and leave behind the lowlands of this world in order to climb out onto the heights, but when you have gained the ridge, the country beneath can be seen and enjoyed, for what it really is, for the first time.[21]

The pilgrimage to Croagh Patrick is one of the most popular forms of asceticism in Ireland, as is the three days spent on the penitential island of Lough Derg, St. Patrick's Purgatory. In medieval times, Lough Derg was one of Europe's major pilgrimage destinations, due to the belief that spending time in the cave on the island would give pilgrims a vision of purgatory and help them live a better life. It used to be a very difficult pilgrimage, since people were locked up there for three days and nights. Now it is only somewhat easier: There is no staying in a cave, but pilgrims have to go barefoot upon reaching the island; they are not allowed to sleep until their second night there; they eat only toast and drink tea; and they constantly pray. Still, the place is packed throughout the pilgrimage months, mostly with young people. Far from being a somber place, it is a place of joy.

Why would people climb a steep mountain, fast several days, or go barefoot on a forsaken isle? Are they imitating their forebears, the ancient Celtic holy men and women, whose ascetical practices were quite severe? For example, it was no unusual thing for men and women to pray for hours with arms outstretched cruciform in the cold flowing waters of the streams of Ireland. It was also expected that the holy men and women would sleep on beds of stone with rocks for pillows. Long fasts were the norm, and even some of the days of the week were named after fasting habits: *Ceadaion* (Wednesday), literally "the first fast;" *An Aoine* (Friday), "the fast;" and *Deardaoin* (Thursday), "the day between the two fasts."[22]

Fasting, especially, was important for monks and laity alike. It was seen as a prayer of adoration—praising God for the beauty of creation. It was seen as a prayer of contrition—a way to say one was truly sorry for sin. Fasting was also used as a thanksgiving for gifts given and as supplication—a physical form of prayer asking God to grant a particular request. Celtic people even used fasting as a means of getting someone to right a wrong, or as a means of exerting moral pressure. St. Patrick, for instance, fasted against a slave owner, and there are even instances of fasting against God himself as this truly wonderful ancient little story testifies:

The abbot of Dairines once saw a little bird weeping and making great lamentation. "O my God," said the abbot, "what has happened to that creature over there?" And with that he swore that he would neither eat nor drink until the cause be revealed to him. He had not long to fast, for an angel soon came that way and said, "Hail

Father! Don't let that question bother you any further.
Molua, the son of Ocha, is dead. And he is mourned by
the creatures, for he never killed any of them, big or
small. So he is mourned by them as much as by humans,
and among those mourners is this little bird that you
see."[23]

Asceticism, which includes all the above disciplines, is done in general for two reasons: one, to do penance for sins committed; two, to subdue the body so that its many desires can be disciplined and the voice of God heard more clearly. The Celtic Christians took seriously what St. Paul said when he urged people to be athletes for Christ:

Do you not know that in a race the runners all compete, but
only one receives the prize? Run in such a way that you
may win it. Athletes exercise self-control in all things; they
do it to receive a perishable wreath, but we an imperish-
able one. So I do not run aimlessly, nor do I box as though
beating the air; but I punish my body and enslave it, so that
after proclaiming to others I myself should not be disquali-
fied. (1 Corinthians 9: 24-27)

Notice that asceticism is never done for its own sake. It means nothing unless directed towards a higher goal. That goal is to conform oneself to the sufferings of Christ. In order to carry the Cross, we have to be in spiritual shape. We will never be able to carry our Cross daily unless we have the spiritual strength necessary to walk with the Lord. There is wisdom here, for often in times past people who practiced asceticism went overboard and increasingly performed harsher and harsher tasks. All good spiritual directors tell us that moderation is what is needed. A person doesn't need to run a marathon every day to be in shape. The same is true with affairs of the spirit. Asceticism is not an end in itself. It exists to help us pray better and see more clearly what God has planned for us.

There is also another secret here, and that is the connection between soul and body. A healthy body and a healthy spirit complement one another. It will be easier to practice asceticism if we are physically in shape, and conversely, if our souls are healthy from good spiritual discipline, chances are good that we will do for our bodies what we do for our souls.

Asceticism is not optional for those who wish to know God. Not only our Christian faith but all religions recognize that the divine cannot be touched or communicated with on an ordinary basis without some form of ascetical practice. The reason is simple. Our minds get clouded with the demands of the body. Of course the body needs and should receive basic nutrition and health care, but our bodies have wants and needs that if not controlled will overwhelm any other pursuit we attempt. Desires for food, sex, leisure and other kinds of visual and auditory stimulation are natural, but if not held in check they take all our time and focus. We really begin to think that there is nothing else to do with life but satisfy our urges and desires. Of course Christianity at times has overreacted to these urges, sometimes condemning any pursuit of them as sinful. Christianity has, however, recognized correctly that we are more than the sum of our bodily or emotional urges and that to achieve what humans are capable of achieving is going to require asceticism. Asceticism does not seek to take the joy out of life. It simply puts everything in its proper perspective.

Most Catholics have forgotten that the Church still places a penitential obligation on its followers. Not just during Lent, but throughout the whole year we are expected to practice at least one ascetical action a week, preferably on Friday, the traditional day of penance. It can be any action of our choice, but done for the right reasons it will be of great help in our attempt to orient ourselves to hear and feel the presence of God.

Meditation

Jesus said, "If any want to become my followers, let them deny themselves and take up their cross daily and follow me. For those who want to save their life will lose it, and those who lose their life for my sake will save it." (Luke 9:23-24)

What does it mean to "carry one's cross daily?" How does a Christian do this in our modern day and age? Jot down the things that make up your personal Cross. How well do you carry it? How can you strengthen yourself or be strengthened by the Lord to carry your Cross better? What acts of penance or asceticism do you already perform in your life? List them and write down how they help you spiritually. If there are none, think about how you might integrate asceticism into your daily life.

Contemplation

You may either do this exercise standing (which is more

difficult) or laying down (which is easier). Extend your arms in the shape of the Cross, saying, "Lord Jesus, I wish to carry my cross daily with joy in my heart. This period of silence I am about to enter, I offer to you. If it be your will, tell me how I may better carry this small sliver of the Cross you bore for me. My heart is open to you. In silence, I am in your presence." Spend some time like this. For those who are standing, you will not be able to endure this long. Don't overdo it. This "praying cruciform" discipline molds our bodies into conformation with Christ on the Cross. It is a method of prayer that demonstrates our oneness with him.

Action

The Church defines fasting as one main meal, plus two smaller meals that together do not exceed the main meal. That is a pretty lenient definition. Some people like to try a more challenging form of fasting. But why should we fast in the first place?

Fasting is a prayer of *adoration*. We are creatures of God, who has a destiny for each one of us, and our fasting prayer adores the Creator.

Fasting is a prayer of *contrition*. We fast because we are sorry for sinning. It is an act of repentance.

Fasting is a prayer of *thanksgiving*. Fasting strips away non-essentials and reminds us that our number one priority in life is God.

Fasting is a prayer of *supplication*. Using both body and soul, we pray for people who need us.

Strictly speaking, fasting means taking certain liquids only. It used to mean just water, but a healthier method is to drink juices and broths in addition to water.

Few people can start out with the above method of fasting. A person has to work up to it. Personal health concerns, age, and good common sense are going to modify the above method so that you can fast to fit your needs. Use the following criteria as a guide:

- Fasting does not mean painful starvation. No one should be able to tell you are fasting.

- Fasting, while uncomfortable at first, should not cause you serious pain. Need some food? Don't worry, eat a little, but don't eat the candy bar. Try some plain bread (with no butter) instead.

- We are not less holy because we cannot keep a strict fast. Be less concerned with the details of fasting and more concerned with the prayerful attitude you maintain.

- Fast for a reason. Use it as one of the prayer forms mentioned above: adoration, contrition, thanksgiving, supplication.

The Celtic Virtue of Sacrament

A Window to God

St. Kevin was walking one day into a valley in the Wicklow Mountains and he came across a lovely glen in which two lakes rested. Glendalough, or the Valley of the Two Lakes, ultimately became a place of great learning and spirituality. But before it was famous, it was Kevin's alone, and there he lived a frugal lifestyle, clad in animal skins, praying to God. So close to the earth and to the Lord he was that the trees would sing to him and all animals watched over him. One day, in the depth of winter after a freshly fallen snow, he walked to the edge of the lake and stood there praying the psalms from his psalter. The psalter fell from his hands and sank into the depths of the lake. Kevin was sorely grieved, for the book was valuable. But an angel appeared to him and told him not to sorrow. Soon, much to Kevin's surprise, an otter appeared with the psalter in its mouth. The book was not wet, not a page was damp, not a letter was smudged.

One year during Lent, Kevin was praying cruciform on his grey flagstone bed. Much to his wonder and joy, a blackbird came and built her nest in his outstretched hand. Consumed with love for one of God's creatures, he did not move throughout Lent and fed only on the heavenly music sung by the angels. An angel came and pleaded with Kevin to cease this penance, but Kevin said, "To hold this blackbird with her young is no great thing, since I do it for the sake of heaven's King, for did not the Christ hold the whole world in his outstretched arms on the cross for the sake of humanity?" And the bird raised her young, and Kevin rejoiced in the Lord.

But the most important event in the glen occurred when the king of the surrounding land sent his young son to be fostered by Kevin. Great was the distress of the king, for all his other sons had been destroyed by the shining people, the fairies. When the king brought his son to Kevin to be baptized, a witch from the shining people stalked the child along with her followers. Determined to kill him as they had all the other king's sons, they appeared before Kevin to snatch the child. But Kevin cursed them and the women were turned to stones. You can still see them on the shores of the lake in the glen—stone witches unable to hurt anyone anymore. Kevin's problems, however, were only just beginning. There was no nurse or midwife, no cows or calves in the glen at that time, and that meant no food for the child. Kevin was in an anxious state, when he looked behind him and saw a doe with her fawn following him. He prayed to God that the doe might be tamed so he might coax milk from it for the child. Immediately the doe walked to the side of a flat rock and dropped her milk in the hollow of a stone so that both the child and her fawn could drink. That stone is reverenced to this very day. Every day the child drank his fill. That place is called Innis Eilte—the doe's milking stand. One day as the doe was grazing, her fawn wandered away. A stray wolf chanced upon it and, being a wolf, devoured the fawn. Kevin chastised the wolf and ordered it to go gently to the doe and act as her fawn. The wolf, in sorrow and repen-

tance, obeyed. The doe continued to drop her milk onto the stone as the wolf stood at her breast, and Kevin took that milk and fed the child until the time he was weaned. The child grew in strength and wisdom and became a disciple of Kevin's. The name of the son of that king is lost to memory, as is the name of the king himself, but St. Kevin's name shines as the stars in the sky, for he that is humble is remembered forever, while the powerful vanish from our minds like the grass that withers and fades.[24]

THE STORY OF ST. KEVIN

No one who immerses themselves in Celtic spirituality can escape the importance the whole of creation plays in the experience of God. There are many stories of saints and their oneness with creation. St. Kevin is the Celtic Francis of Assisi, and many others like him learned great things about God from their relationship with the created denizens of the world. There is always an innocence and a sense of humor in these stories. Take St. Colman and his three pets: a rooster, a mouse and a fly. Each morning the rooster would crow, waking Colman for his prayers. The fly would walk across the page of his psalter marking Colman's place, for the old man could no longer see very well. When he began to doze at his prayers, the little mouse would nibble on his ear to bring him back to an awareness of God. When the three animals died, St. Colman was so heartbroken that St. Columba himself had to chastise him and remind him that the creatures belonged not to him but to the Lord.

These types of stories were told by the Celts to relate how the saints by their holiness recreated the relationship that Adam and Eve had with nature before the fall of humanity. Besides being enjoyable tales, they reiterate the ability of humans—with the grace of God—to once again be in harmony with creation. These stories bring home the truth that we must live in peace with the earth if we are to be one with God. We are given the use of the world and its creatures, but we must take care of the treasure and not exploit it.

"Stewardship of creation" is similar to environmentalism, but different in one key way. It focuses on another virtue that Celtic spirituality knows well: the religious virtue of *sacrament*. We're not talking about the Seven Sacraments here. This is sacrament with a small "s." It refers to the value of seeing creation as a window to God, as having the ability to reveal qualities and characteristics of the God we worship. Nature is holy, not because it is God, but because it is able to link us to God. As the psalmist says, "The heavens proclaim the glory of God and the firmament shows forth the work of his hands. Day unto day takes up the story and night unto night makes known the message." (Psalm 19:2-3) Creation becomes a window to God when we see that each creature has a quality of God encapsulated in it. For instance, dogs and birds and other animals reflect aspects of God that humans do not. Mountains and lakes have characteristics as well that, when properly appreciated, can lead us to God.

It is this Celtic way of seeing God in creation, of treasuring and preserving the harmony that should exist, that helps us better understand the Catholic emphasis on the sacramental nature of the world. We Catholics believe that though sin has entered the world, sin never destroyed our human nature or the goodness of creation entirely. In fact, we say that though weak, people are still good; though fallen, people still have a window to God through creation. It's really important to grasp this notion, for when people want to know what makes a Catholic a Catholic it is this: We believe that sin did not destroy our essential goodness. It weakened it, certainly, but Christ came to save us because we were worth being saved. This is different from what Martin Luther, John Calvin and others of the Protestant Reformation thought. They taught that when Adam and Eve sinned, human beings became essentially evil, as did all creation. Man-made things or human beings could not be windows to God. We were too corrupt. Many of their followers today no longer subscribe completely to these views, but Luther and Calvin's theologies have heavily influenced certain strains of Christianity down to this day. So important are these distinctions that it is worth fleshing them out a bit more.

The Catholic view of human beings and the world goes like this: Our view of human beings is basically optimistic. When humanity sinned in the dim mists of time, we became weak because of sin. But still, down deep, we were capable of doing and being good with God's grace. This grace, which is God's strength, this love and presence in our lives, lifts us up and helps us achieve our potential, building on the good already there. Of course, God has not restored us to our former perfection. Even creation has fallen with us. Sin has harmed the world, but it has not utterly corrupted it. When we look at what Jesus did for us, we discover that he suffered and died for us precisely because God *loves* the world.

Now the alternative view, held by many non-Catholic theologies both past and present and some extreme radical forms of Catholicism (like Jansenism, the Catholic version of Puritanism), sees the world differently. Here the view of human beings is basically pessimistic: When original sin touched humanity, it utterly corrupted us, made us inherently evil. Down deep, people are bad. And because we are completely corrupted by sin, we are incapable of doing any good; in fact, we are incapable of even cooperating with God's grace: Any good we do is God's doing. We really don't have anything to do with it; all goodness in us is God working through us. In this theological world view, grace covers up wickedness and we are incapable of cooperating with God. Sin has corrupted not only humanity, but nature as well. It, too, has no spark of goodness in it. In this view, Christ saves us on the Cross despite our evil, despite our sinfulness.

An image that will help us see the dichotomy is to picture two architects who walk into the forest and see the ruins of an old Georgian colonial home. The Celtic architect would say, "Look at this old house; see the beautiful columns. What it once must have been! There is still beauty here; we will restore it to its former greatness." In other words, grace fills up what is lacking. The other architect would respond, "Look at this old house, what a ruin. It is beyond repair. We'll gut it, cover up its ugliness, and build something new in its place." In other words, grace covers up ruin and evil.

These antithetical views have monumental consequences on how we live. The Celtic sacramental view of the world plays out practically in this fashion. Since a human being is made in God's image and likeness, and since that image has not been destroyed but only weakened by sin, it follows that a person is a reflection of God and that person's relationships are also a reflection of God's relationship with us. If that is true, then it is not enough to have a personal relationship only with God, important as that is, because it is through relationships with others that God speaks to us. A healthy spiritual life involves not only a personal relationship with Jesus Christ, but also a healthy relationship with oneself and with others. It is a triangular relationship in which health, both spiritual and physical, is measured by how we relate to others. That is why marriage is a sacrament for Catholics. Good in itself, it has been ennobled by Christ as a real way in which God speaks to us through the love of husband and wife. After all, does not Scripture say that God is love? When a couple loves each other deeply, they discover a deeper relationship with God, and when their personal relationship with Christ is healthy, they love each other more.

We can go even further with this. Because Creation has not lost all its original goodness, it too can communicate the presence of God. Suddenly, simple things of the earth—water, oil, human touch, bread, wine—can transmit the presence of God. This is the power of sacraments, and only a person with a sacramental view can truly understand this. That is why our churches—even the most modern, stripped-down versions—use statues, stained glass windows, holy water and crucifixes to communicate the presence of God. In a Catholic Church, one's senses should be assaulted with the presence of God. In a sacramental view, this is done so that we might be instantly reminded of the nearness of God. Of course this view is easily misunderstood by those not of our faith and sometimes misused by those in our faith. If material things begin to obscure the presence of God and we focus solely on the things of this world, then we have lost perspective. Even with that caveat, however, the risk is worth it, for as the poet Gerard Manly Hopkins writes, "The world is charged with the grandeur of God!"

But there is even more. Since we discover God in relationships, the community of the Church becomes more than just a gathering of people. It becomes a divine institution, because God is the center of this community. Catholics have always been known to be a church-oriented people. Our sacramental view, which is strongly influenced by the Celts, tells why. There is no such thing as a solitary Catholic. We need each other in order to be truly healthy. The institution of the Church is not some corporate structure but a dynamic living people united in their journey towards God. It is important that we remember that our faith is not just a private thing between God and ourselves. It involves those around us as well. "For where two or three are gathered in my name," says Christ, "I am there among them." (Matthew 18:20) In a world where creation is holy and we can see the face of Christ in everyone we meet, the Church exists.

In the traditional Protestant view, humanity and the world cannot be sacraments because nothing can transmit the presence of God. Nothing created is good enough. All is corrupted. This has practical consequences in the practice of faith: Human relationships are, of course, to be valued, but they have been too tainted by sin to be able to transmit God's presence in a sacramental way. While friendships are important, they do not reveal God to us. While marriage is a natural bond, even blessed by God, it cannot reveal God to us. What is most important, and indeed, the only sure thing, is one's personal relationship with Jesus Christ and one's willingness to be convicted at the foot of the Cross, surrendering all to Jesus.

The created world is similarly handicapped. The things of the world cannot be doorways to God. Thus in most Protestant churches there is a simplicity and austerness not found in those churches with sacramental views: little stained glass, no statues, no holy water, no crucifix (perhaps only a cross). Even in the large non-denominational evangelical churches, the interior of the building is more like a stage with theater seating. The suspicion of "things" is paramount in this world view—a world view that would have been incomprehensible to the Celts.

Often we see distinctions like this as sectarian. But in our quest for Christian unity, we cannot forget that real differences came out of the Reformation. Pretending those are not present does little to further our unity. Yet it must be said that in the churches of the Reformation there is a real breakdown of barriers occurring. The sacramental view of Catholicism, which is very prevalent in Celtic spirituality, has been taken up by more and more people, particularly in the Anglican (Episcopalian), Lutheran, Methodist and Presbyterian communities. Perhaps the scars of time are healing and a balance is being restored.

Beyond the sectarian squabbles lies a deeper truth. The sacramental view of the world, of nature, of all Creation, resonates in the hearts of all people. How often have we heard of men and women who have left the practice of any faith still finding solace and deep spiritual meaning listening to music or walking in the woods? Even an atheist who appreciates art, music and nature betrays his or her innate sacramental nature. All things point to God, all things lead to God, all things are reflections of God's presence—most especially human beings, who do not simply reflect but are made in the image of their Creator.

Meditation

Celtic spirituality has always valued nature as an easy way to get in touch with God. Celtic monks were always very much involved with the world, but when they needed a spiritual lift they would forsake the monastery and go to an out-of-the-way place, a *diseart* (desert) of their own choosing. Amidst the wild beauty of Scotland, Ireland and Wales it was simple to be in touch with God. The holy places of the Celts were always natural places: a grove of oaks, a holy well, a cliff face above the pounding sea. For many of us, especially those who live in urban areas, it is more difficult to find places like this. Often we have to craft our own: a corner of our house, a little garden in the backyard, even just a few plants on an apartment porch. Why, it is difficult for many of us to even see the night sky! When was the last time you let nature reveal God to you? Is nature just a thing to be used, or do you walk the world aware of the human obligation to care for the earth? Do you have a care for the land and the animals and plants that inhabit it? Take a moment and write down the last time nature helped reveal God to you. It may have been an experience on a trip, or with a pet, or on a walk, but recall it and write down how creation revealed God to you and what that revelation consisted of.

Contemplation

Go sit somewhere with nature and simply become aware of the divine presence. No need to worry how this period of prayer will go. Having reflected on past events where God has revealed himself to you through the world, quiet yourself and listen.

Action

To simply be connected to the earth because it is trendy to do so now is not Celtic spirituality. One has to have a sense that all creation can communicate the presence of God. This sense has to be overt and conscious. An atheist appreciating beauty may in actuality be saluting God, but the action does nothing for the atheist since he or she has closed off that avenue. What do you need to do to be connected to creation? What is one action a week you can carry out to bring to mind your place in the universe in a way that helps you appreciate the beauty around you? Plan it and do it.

The Celtic Virtues of Community and Hope

We Are Not Alone

O angel of God who has charge of me,
From the dear Father of mercifulness,
Put 'round about me this night,
The embracing love of heaven's saints.

Drive from me every temptation and danger,
Surround me in times of confusion and weakness,
And in my waking, working and sleeping,
Keep safe my life,
Guard me always.

Be a bright flame before me,
Be a smooth path beneath me,
Be a kindly shepherd beside me,
Today, tonight and forever.

For I am tired,
A stranger on earth's shore.
Lead me to the land of the angels.
For I yearn to go home,
To the peace of Christ,
To the hope of heaven.[25]

PRAYER TO THE GUARDIAN ANGEL

Brigid of Kildare was the daughter of an Irish chieftain and at an early age pledged herself to Christ. Totally dedicated to the people of the land, she became a great abbess and was known for her powers of healing and generosity. The following is from the Lives of the Saints in the ancient Book of Lismore.[26]

For everything that Brigid would ask of the Lord was granted her at once. For this was her desire: to satisfy the poor, to expel every hardship, to spare every miserable man. Now there never has been anyone more demure, or more modest, or more gentle, or more humble, or wiser, or more harmonious than Brigid. She never washed her hands, her feet or her head among men. She never looked at the face of a man. She never would speak without blushing. She was abstinent, she was innocent, she was prayerful, she was patient; she was glad in God's commandments; she was firm, she was humble, she was forgiving, she was loving; she was a consecrated casket for keeping Christ's Body and his Blood; she was a temple of God. Her heart and her mind were a throne of rest for the Holy Ghost. She was simple towards God; she was compassionate towards the wretched; she was splendid in miracles and marvels; wherefore her name among created things is Dove among birds, Vine among trees, Sun among stars. This is the father of that holy virgin, the Heavenly Father; this is her son, Jesus Christ; this is her fosterer, the Holy Ghost; wherefore this holy virgin performs great marvels and innumerable miracles. It is she who helps everyone who is in difficulty or in danger; it is she that abates the pestilence; it is she that quells the anger and the storm of the sea. She is the prophetess of Christ; she is the Queen of the South; she is the Mary of the Gael.

IN PRAISE OF ST. BRIGID

⸻

I t appears that many of today's Catholics unfortunately forget that our faith is not just a private thing between God and ourselves; it involves those around us as well. Christ tells us that he is even more present when a community gathers, which is a major reason for the existence of the Church. In a world where creation is holy and we can see the face of Christ in everyone we meet, the Church exists. The Church is all those who believe, united around the Pope and bishops, together in faith with each other. That idea is very easy for Catholics to remember, but many forget something just as important: We are not alone. Our loved ones do not cease to exist after death, and death itself is not a barrier. There are also other beings created by God who exist and occasionally have dealings with humanity, namely the angels. The ancient Celtic Christian took all of this for granted. After all, do we not say at Mass just before the Holy Holy, "And so with all the saints and angels we proclaim our song of joy…." Celtic spirituality brings home the fact that when the Eucharist is celebrated, it is not just those of us in the pews who pray, but all those holy ones who have gone before us and are now around the throne of God, as well as those messengers of

God, the holy angels.

Chief of those who make up the "invisible cloud of witnesses" is Mary, the Mother of God. She was a very attractive figure to the Celts for she not only embodied the feminine side of creation but also helped them understand the divinity and humanity of Christ, as well as his purpose in walking among us. We get our first hint that death is not a barrier when we realize that Mary was assumed body and soul into heaven. Mary has always been the revealer of Christ. What we say about her says something even more powerful about Jesus. For example, what does the Assumption mean? Simply this: God keeps his promises. The Resurrection would have been astounding and tremendous had it only happened to Christ, but ultimately it would have proved disappointing to us. Perhaps it was a one-time event. Christ, however, said that his faithful people would not be left alone. They would live with him forever. What happened to Christ was not an isolated event. Mary, the most perfect follower of our Lord, was gifted immediately with what we one day hope to have happen to us. We too shall rise from the dead, if we remain faithful to the Lord as Mary did.

Mary was loved by the Celts because she brought the intimacy and closeness of the Divinity to them. She gave humanity the Lord, and Celtic spirituality treasures that truth. She is the greatest of the saints, but by no means the only one honored. The saints were not distant beings whose dim memory was celebrated by the Celts. The Celts viewed these saints as holy men and women who happened to have died but still remained close, effective helpers who were busy with the daily life of human beings. Columba died near the beginning of the seventh century, for example, but the fisherman from the Outer Hebrides in the last century felt him as closely as the monks whom Columba served over a thousand years before.

These men and women were powerful. Take Brigid, for instance—she rode around on her chariot helping men and women, healing lepers and the ill, arguing with kings, and generally getting her way. The story at the start of this chapter shows how she is remembered. Her sense of humor and compassion are legendary. So great was Brigid that she eclipsed an old Celtic goddess of the same name. A lovely story exists of how she founded the abbey of Kildare. The local king was reluctant to give her any land, so she smiled and said, "I do not need much; how about as much land as I can spread a blanket over?" The king thought this a splendid deal and agreed. But much to his chagrin, he stood speechless as Brigid gathered four of her sisters and told them to each grab an end of the blanket. "Run my sisters!" she cried, "Run!" And run they did. The blanket simply grew in size. Soon the sisters were out of sight. Finally the king got his voice back and begged Brigid to stop. She did and thanked the king for the excellent gift of land.

Many people seem to think that the age of saints is over. Not so. Brigid is still honored. Remember the description of St. Brigid's Well in the Burren? It is still a popular site among locals and tourists alike. One cannot forget the friends of God so easily.

A lot of people, including Catholics, ask why we even need saints anymore. The answer is clear: because we are only human. Blessed Mother Teresa, for example, is rapidly on her way to becoming formally declared a saint. In life she was a tireless worker for the poor and everyone who came to her for help. God worked through this woman, tangibly, effectively. When she died, do you think she became powerless? Our faith tells us that holy men and women enjoy God's presence eternally. They are perfected. Mother Teresa, in fact, should be even more helpful now than before. What in life was simply asking her to do a favor, becomes—now that she is undoubtedly in heaven—a prayer to her for help.

Praying to the saints to ask them to continue doing from heaven what they did so well on earth is a natural thing, not idolatrous at all. Critics of this practice say, "All we need is Jesus." Of course that is true. Before earth or the universe existed, there was only God. God was all that was needed. But God wanted to love and share that love with others, and so came creation. The friends of God are family, and we get to know a lot about God by knowing the sons and daughters he made. Do we have to pray to saints? No. But our lives can be enriched if we do.

In our sacramental faith people—as well as nature—can be windows to God. There is no need to be isolated in this life. The Celtic belief in the virtue of *community*, the idea that the real world is made up of both the physical and spiritual realms, is most clearly seen here. Mary, angels and saints are friends, partners on the journey. "Who are these wearing white robes, and where did they come from?...These are the ones who have survived the time of great distress; they have washed their robes and made them white in the blood of the Lamb. For this reason they stand before God's throne and worship him day and night in his temple." (Revelation 7:14-15)

Angels, like saints, surround us. Many people, however, have a misconception of them. They are the messengers of God and they are not human, but they are not cute-looking cherubs with wings. They are totally distinct and separate beings whom we occasionally encounter in life, though most often we are not aware of their presence. Many stories exist about the saints being surrounded by angels. St. Columba, for example, is especially well known for this.

On the island of Iona, there is a small hill rising just above a *machair* (a grassy pasture by the sea). Today, it is covered with green grass and a farmer's shed is at the base of it, but traditionally it has been known as the Hill of the Angels, for this is where St. Columba was observed praying in the midst of angels—celestial beings in human form that flew to him, stood around him, and conversed with him. So says St. Adamnan, a near contemporary chronicler of Columba's life. What is meant by the tale is no mere vision but instead a factual account of how close the spiritual world is to us.

We were all taught as children that we have a guardian angel. Jesus told us we have one (see Matthew 18:10), but unfortunately many of us ditched our guardian angels right about the same time we got rid of our childhood imaginary friends. Most of us have not thought about this ever-present guardian for years, but perhaps that is because we refuse to see angels for what they really are.

Why are they important? First of all, they function as messengers of God. The word "angel" means messenger. They can bring us news from God. One needs only to think about the Angel Gabriel's announcing the birth of Christ to Mary. Angels also communicate divine knowledge and love. They are reminders of

God's concern for humanity. The story of the Archangel Raphael and the boy Tobias in the Old Testament Book of Tobit is a great example of this. Angels remind us that humanity is not alone. We don't need to be looking for aliens, for Christians already know that human beings aren't the only intelligent creatures in the universe. Angels also protect humanity from evil. The great story of St. Michael appearing in Rome with a flaming sword, bowing to Pope St. Gregory fifteen hundred years ago as the Pope prayed for deliverance of the city from the plague, is just one of many instances of angels protecting humans.

In fact, St. Michael is quite beloved of the Celts. Skellig Michael, a towering island once home to a famous monastery and still seen as a place of pilgrimage, looms eight miles off the southwestern coast of Ireland. Michael is seen as a protector of Ireland and master of the wind and waves. In Scotland, particularly on the Outer Hebridean Islands, Michaelmas Day on September 29 is very important. St. Michael's bread was baked on that day, graves of the dead were blessed, matchmaking took place among the young, and God was given thanks for the incoming harvest.

Angels as guardians is not just a childish notion. The sophisticated guardian angel prayer at the beginning of this chapter comes from the Island of Barra in the Outer Hebrides. There are many forms of this prayer, but its updated version serves us well by reminding us that God has placed an angelic spirit to guide and guard us. Celtic spirituality makes us realize that there is more to reality than just the visible world.

Whenever we are tempted to doubt the relevance of the Church and its importance, whenever we find ourselves more isolated than we like, it is good to remember how interconnected we are. Our baptism initiated us into this grand community. The Church community is more than God, the angels, the saints and those of us still alive. After all, not all those who have passed on are saints. Thus we pray for the dead, and we only do that because we know that many, perhaps most of us, die with unfinished business.

At the moment of death, many of us have yet to let go of our angers, lusts or jealousies, and we cannot see the face of God until we let go of that which keeps us tied to imperfection. This belief, called purgatory, received much of its concrete imagery from Celtic Christianity. Far from being the waiting room of hell, it is simply that place or state of being where we let go of that which makes us imperfect. Celtic spirituality, just like Catholic belief in general, holds that those in purgatory need our prayers. The Celts, however, were not content to let purgatory be an intellectual concept. After all, these souls were their dear-departed loved ones. The pagan Celts believed that on October 31 the spiritual and material worlds were especially intertwined and the dead walked the earth. The Celts would often wear masks so the dead would not recognize them. From that practice came our own wearing of costumes on Halloween. When the Church Christianized the Celts and gave them a more positive view of the afterlife, the Celts embraced those new notions while keeping the old. They still celebrated the Eve of All Saints (Halloween), but encouraged by the Church they remembered the holy ones on All Saints Day, November 1, and their departed loved ones who still needed their prayers on All Souls Day, November 2.

The Celtic people's appreciation of the afterlife existed before they were converted to Christianity. Death held no real fear for them. Christianity bolstered that view and added the belief that Christ was stronger than all powers of evil. In fact, this very truth may have made it very easy for the Celts to convert. The Church gave them an even stronger hope that the dead would see God. Concretely, that means those in purgatory—those with unfinished business—are assured of salvation but need our prayers of strength to let go of imperfection. The "poor souls" complete the circle of community for the Celtic Christian. Just as we rely on the saints to pray for us, so we pray for the dead. That pattern demonstrates that we are all tied together. That's why death for a Christian is difficult and tough, but not horrific and terrible. It is a passing, not a ceasing. It is a beginning, not an ending. Our very self, our individuality, is not annihilated by death, nor does death conquer love. This wonderful awareness of community gives birth to another virtue, that of *hope*. We walk with one foot in this world and the other in the spiritual realm. Of course there is sorrow here in this life. People die tragically and there is much pain. Yet beneath all that sadness is a deep, pulsating joy. It is the joy Christ gave us in his resurrection: the assurance that death is not the final part of our story and that we will never walk this road of life and death alone.

Meditation

Who are the heroes in your life? Think for a moment about who you have admired and looked up to during your life. What characteristics and qualities did these people have? Now answer this question: Were they holy? Remember, it is not enough just to be good; a saint is extraordinary. Chances are, the people you have looked up to have been good people with many qualities of holiness. They have given you a glimpse of God by the way they have treated you or lived their lives. Saints are the major league versions of those good and noble people. Perhaps one of those people you have thought of does fit that extraordinary category, but you have most likely not met a true saint. And yet, they do exist and should be called upon by us for help and companionship. Most Christians were baptized or confirmed with a saint's name. Have you talked with your patron saint lately, prayed to him or her, asked for help and guidance? Perhaps it is time to find new saintly role models for your current stage in life. What are the struggles and crises currently facing you? Write them down. If possible, grab a book of saints (there are many versions at your religious goods store or local book store) and look for one who had to struggle as you have to struggle. Strike up a prayerful conversation with that saint. This should not be strange to a sacramentally charged Christian. We are surrounded by that "invisible cloud of witnesses." They are there to help and guide us. Speak to them. Use their wisdom. Ask them to help you.

Contemplation

Go to your parish church either early before Sunday Mass or at some other quiet time. Look at the Presence Light burning before the tabernacle where Jesus is present. Acknowledge the Lord. Look around the church and study the statues or windows that depict the saints of God. Now look at the altar. This is where the Eucharist takes place, a sacrifice, a memorial, a meal where Christ becomes present. When the Mass approaches the moment when the bread and wine become the body and blood of Christ, the priest asks us to join with "all the saints and angels" in a song of joy, and we sing "Holy, Holy, Holy." Recall that moment, and in the silence of the church become aware that you are not alone. Christ is with you, the saints are with you, the angels are with you. Simply rest in their presence for a while.

Action

Some daily routines need to be instituted to constantly bring to mind the fact that we do not walk this world separated from heaven. First, have a few favorite saints to speak to. Think of it as having a spiritual coffee break with them. Become familiar in your prayerful conversations with them. It is all a part of getting to know the Lord's family. Second, rather than get sucked into the trendy, new-age fascination with angels, begin again to pray to your guardian angel on a regular basis. Third, if you do not already have a deep devotion to the Mother of God, now is the time to start. Rediscover the rosary and pray it.

The Celtic Virtues of Word and Eucharist

In the Presence
of the Lord

Sean Maloney was a petty thief, a common thing during the bad times 300 years ago when the Irish were oppressed by the British and the Catholic faith was banned. All priests were considered fugitives to be killed on sight, and with no one to say Mass the people could not gather for prayer.

One day Sean was caught stealing. The penalty for theft in those days was death. Before he was to hang, the sheriff noticed something about him—a hardness, a viciousness, a darkness perhaps that would suit the sheriff's purposes. He offered Sean his life, but only if he became a priest hunter— someone who would hunt and kill the priests who were still hiding in the land giving the sacraments to the people. "You'll kill the priests and bring me their heads," said the sheriff. "And I'll give you your life plus a gold piece for each head."

"Agreed," said Sean Maloney, and from that day forward he was no longer known as Sean Maloney, petty thief, but Sean na'Sagart—Sean the Priest Hunter.

From Westport to Ballintubber to Cong—all over the western part of Ireland—Sean hunted priests and killed them. He would take their heads and run through the towns saying, "I can live a little longer, the rent is paid!" And he'd collect his reward—a gold piece for each priest's head. How many priests did he kill? Well, not far from Ballintubber Abbey is a little lake surrounded by dark green trees. Its dark waters hold many secrets. It is called the Lake of the Heads. Sean na'Sagart visited it many times.

In Westport, he hunted a priest named Fr. LaVelle and shot him as the priest was trying to escape in a boat. Terrible as that murder was, it was that death that started the hand of God moving closer to Sean na'Sagart, for the priest's nephew vowed revenge and began stalking the priest hunter.

There came a day when Sean was in the vicinity of Ballintubber Abbey. He went to his sister, Nancy, and told her he was mortally sick, that he had had a change of heart and wished to be forgiven for his sins before he died. Nancy, a good and faithful Catholic woman, didn't know how black the heart of Sean na'Sagart was, for Sean was using one of his old tricks. After all, what priest would refuse to come to the aid of a dying sinner?

And so Nancy ran across the field to the church at Ballintubber Abbey and told Father Kilger and Father Burke that Sean was near death. Now both priests suspected a trick, and Father Kilger, who was old, insisted over the younger priest's objections that he should go. He had lived his life already, and if it was a trick it was better to lose a priest who would die soon anyway, rather than a young priest who had years of service ahead of him.

It was a trick. Nancy led old Father Kilger back to her home, and he found Sean laying with his face to the wall. "Father, I'm glad you've come," wheezed Sean. "I need to make my confession." The priest knelt down by Sean's bedside and said, "Are you sorry for your sins, my son?" But instead of feeling sorrow breaking out of the soul of the sinner Sean na'Sagart, the priest felt only the cold dagger enter his body and sever the thread of his life. With his hand upraised for absolution, Father Kilger was murdered in cold blood.

That evening Sean was drinking with his soldier friends. He was always guarded now, for the sheriff found him very valuable and didn't want anything to happen to the best priest hunter he had. Now Johnny McCann, nephew of the murdered priest from Westport, had been hunting Sean. He had disguised himself as a peddler and was in the tavern when Sean came in boasting that he had killed Father Kilger and taken his head. Sean began to make fun of Johnny and the soldiers joined in. Even Johnny laughed at himself and played the fool. But this peddler was no fool. He had found the priest hunter, and now he only had to wait till Sean was alone. Sean became drunk, and the peddler was able to take Sean's knife and empty the powder out of his gun. Johnny went to Father Burke and told him that Sean would be waiting for him when he went to bury Father Kilger the next day. He gave Father Burke Sean's knife.

The next day Father Kilger was to be buried. It was the custom in those troubled and dangerous times to disguise the priest who would be present at the funeral as an old hag, and so young Father Burke was there, grief stricken, hunched over like an old crone to secretly bless the body of his friend and pastor. But Sean na'Sagart was there too, and he spied the old hag and guessed it was a young priest in disguise. He *unmasked Father Burke and was about to execute him there in the cemetery. He pulled out his pistol, placed it next to the temple of Father Burke and squeezed the trigger. Having no powder, the gun couldn't fire, and in the commotion Father Burke escaped.*

And so began a race for life and death. Father Burke took off over the fields with Sean na'Sagart close behind. Out in the fields, the priest hunter closed in on his victim. A root tripped the priest and he fell, injuring his leg. The priest looked back and saw the face of death come closer. Sean na'Sagart laughed and threw himself upon the priest, trying to beat him to death with the butt of his pistol. But Johnny McCann had followed also and cried out to the priest, "The knife, Father, the knife!" And Father Burke in desperation pulled out Sean's own knife and stabbed him in the side. Sean gasped in pain and rolled off the priest as Johnny McCann rushed up and seized the knife and stabbed the priest hunter to death, avenging his dead uncle and saving the life of Father Davy Burke.

The people of the area dragged the body of Sean to the lake behind Ballintubber Abbey and threw it in the water. But Father Burke ordered that it be brought to the cemetery and given a burial, arguing that Father Kilger had most assuredly forgiven the priest hunter and the people should do the same. The people may have forgiven Sean, but they didn't forget. There in the cemetery, all the graves face the east, where Christ rose from the dead and where he will come again. All the graves face east except one—the grave of Sean na'Sagart. He was buried facing north, the way pagans were buried, for he showed no sign of repentance, no fear of God, no sorrow for sin. No flowers were ever placed on his grave. It was shunned and spurned. Years later a tree grew there and split his grave. The descendants of those brave people worship in peace and joy today, for to those who suffer and die for their faith goes the victory, while those who persecute the faithful of Christ lie forsaken in their broken graves.[27]

THE STORY OF SEAN NA'SAGART

nyone visiting beautiful Ballintubber Abbey, now the parish church of the region, is struck not only by the haunting immediacy of the penal days when the Catholic faith was outlawed—days three hundred years in the past but still fresh in the minds of the people—but also by the enduring faith of the folk and their love for the Eucharist. The church was only roofed in the middle of the last century, so for nearly 400 years, ever since Cromwell destroyed much of the church, Mass was always celebrated in the roofless church regardless of the weather.

The importance of **Word** and **Eucharist** is central to Celtic spirituality. In the early days of Christianity in Ireland, it was love and knowledge of Scriptures that made up preparation for priestly ministry.[28] Monks would routinely memorize all 150 psalms and recite them daily. In a society that valued oral tradition, such a feat was quite normal. Laity would not be expected to do this, but love for the Scriptures was transmitted to them through the sermons at Mass and even through the exquisite pictures carved into the High Crosses. And, of course, there was the grand tradition of illuminating manuscripts, which gave the world an art form never seen before. Painstakingly copied, collections of the Scriptures, such as *The Book of Kells,* would enhance the words copied by their art. The added pictures, the detailed rendering of a single letter beginning a book or even a page, demonstrates to this day the love the Celtic people had for the Word of God. Spoken or read, the Word communicated the presence of Christ and served as the guide for daily life. Yet, the Word cannot be separated from its crucial context—that of the Eucharist. There it received its most profound expression and treatment. For the Celts the Scriptures and the Eucharist went together.

In these days of splintered Christendom, love for the Scriptures unites all denominations. There is little animosity left in this area. All Christians recognize that the Scriptures transmit the living legacy of God's love for us. For some, that is enough. But not for Catholics. Like the ancient Celtic Christians, Catholics know the intimate connection between Word and Eucharist. Our experience of the Bible is, as it was for the Celts, primarily an aural one. We *hear* the Scriptures more than we read them. Of course the Bible should be read privately, but for Catholics the dynamic nature of the Word comes alive at Sunday Mass. The Word forms us, whets our appetite for an even closer experience of God. It points the way to the primary experience of God that we have: namely, the Eucharist.

Jesus says, "I am the bread of life; whoever comes to me will never hunger, and whoever believes in me will never thirst." (John 6:35) As important as that statement is, modern Catholics seem to have a difficult time understanding what the Eucharist means for them. For the first 1,000 years of Christianity, what and who was received at Communion was never in doubt. People simply believed that they were receiving Christ. Yet the second 1,000 years of our faith has seen the Church splintered over this very question. Now even Catholics seem confused. Some believe they simply receive bread and wine at Mass; others believe that in some way a spiritual presence of Christ is there, but it is still basically bread and wine. Still others believe that it is really Christ if they think it is and it is not if they don't. But the Church's teaching is the same today as it was 2,000 years ago: The bread and wine, though they retain the outward form and taste of bread and wine, are changed into the Body and Blood of Jesus Christ. No longer bread and wine, they are Christ. It is what Catholics call the "Real Presence." No other faith makes a claim to come this close to God.

Many non-Catholics cannot understand why they cannot receive Communion at Mass. Many Protestant churches have no trouble with intercommunion. Everyone is welcome. But their perspective is different. For many of them, all one receives is bread and wine. What's the big problem? Even if an unbeliever should come forward there would be no sacrilege. But that is not the perspective of Catholics. First of all, *communion* is a Latin word meaning "in union with." For a person to come forward at Mass to receive Communion means that person is saying, "I agree with this Church, what they believe and how they believe it." But what if they really do not believe; what if they have no intention of belonging to this Church? It may look and feel nice, but no one should come up to *receive* God unless they really believe it *is* God. If they truly believe that, then they should take the steps necessary to join the Church that offers such a gift. Conversely, for a Catholic to receive communion in another denomination is really not right either. Knowingly or not, that person is saying he or she agrees with what the non-Catholic community is saying about its communion. One of the core issues that split the Church in the Reformation was the issue of the Mass and the Eucharist, and until we resolve those major issues there will always be a sadness that all Christians cannot come to the same altar to receive our Lord.

When the English were persecuting the Irish and forbidding them to have Mass, the people held on strongly to their beliefs. Priests would say Mass at "Mass Rocks" in the fields so that people could have the Eucharist. The most uneducated Irish peasant knew instinctively that he or she needed the Eucharist. Today many of us take the gift that we have for granted. We will run here and there to some reported miracle—a statue weeping, a vision seen—but we will ignore the greatest miracle of all: the presence of Christ in the Eucharist.

It is striking to remember that John's Gospel was written to help emphasize the importance of the Eucharist. With all the witnesses to Christ's life dying off, everyone was worried that no one would be able to tell the stories and remember Jesus. John spoke forcefully and firmly through his Gospel that sacraments were going to be the way to stay intimately connected with Jesus, and the Eucharist would be the best, most consistent path to true communion with Christ.

How can we deepen our appreciation for the Eucharist? The Mass is obviously a meal and a memorial, but in order to really appreciate the presence of Christ in the Eucharist, we must once again see the Eucharist as sacrifice. Here is how to envision what this means to us: Jesus died on the cross 2,000 years ago to save us. The Father accepted the worthiness of this sacrifice and raised his Son from the dead. This is the whole death/resurrection event to which the Scriptures testify. Jesus now sits at the right hand of the Father. Since eternity is an eternal "now," the Father still is ratifying that sacrifice of Christ. When we say that Jesus "sits at the right hand of the Father," that means the Father is still accepting his Son. The Father says, "What you did on the Cross continues." That's why salvation is not just a past event. It happens every day. What good would the Crucifixion or the Resurrection be if these were simply memories? No, in order for us to be touched now, those same events have to be continuing. Otherwise, how are we going to experience salvation?

When we come together as Church, we are the Body of Christ. St. Paul was very clear throughout his letters that when the Church gathers, Christ is present in a special way. We become part of him. At the altar, we say, 'We want to be a part of the saving event you did for us, Lord; we do what you asked us to do; as we remember what you did for us, we offer ourselves with this bread and wine.'

And the Father, who eternally accepts his Son's sacrifice, sees our desire to be united with Christ and accepts us. The Eucharist becomes a bridge between eternity and history: God reaches in and makes us a part of something that happened 2,000 years ago and is still occurring in eternity. The Crucifixion, the tomb, the Resurrection, the Ascension, all become part of *our* experience. We are there—not back in Jerusalem some 2,000 years ago—but as that event continues to exist with God. The bread and wine become Christ's body and blood, and when God accepts our humble gifts and they become Christ, we become part of his sacrifice. The Cross becomes a present event for us, and for a moment we experience Christ's resurrected glory.

So when we say the Mass is a sacrifice, we mean that we are committing ourselves to the one sacrifice of Christ and taking part in his Cross and Resurrection. By joining ourselves with Christ, we take part in the Christ event. Our sins are forgiven and we experience salvation now, this present moment.

Why is a priest necessary? He represents Christ in the offering of the sacrifice, and he stands as the designated leader of the community who brings us together to unite as a Church in prayer with God. He also prepares the Eucharist, which is refreshment to us. Often Catholics are asked, "Have you experienced Jesus as your personal Lord and Savior?" Of course, the correct answer is, "Yes, of course. Every time I receive Jesus in Communion I experience him as my Lord and Savior."

This was the bedrock experience of the Celtic Christian, and it continues to be our experience today.

That's why going to Mass is so important for a Catholic. Without the Eucharist we starve. Without the community experience we are lost. We find our identity and our spiritual meaning around the table of the Lord. We need to be with a spiritual family that has a destiny. We need the Eucharist because we sin and need to be healed. And since the Eucharist is real food, we know it gives us the strength we need to live as Christ wishes us to live.

There is a joy and optimism that comes from all of this, and a realization of the important relationship between priest and people. The Irish always had a great love for the Mass. It grew even stronger when the Mass was outlawed by the occupying British. There were a whole series of delightful Celtic prayers to be said walking on the way to Mass. Here is one titled "King of the Blessed Sunday":

> *A hundred welcomes to you, O King of the Blessed*
> *   Sunday*
> *Who has come to help us after the week.*
> *Guide my feet early to Mass,*
> *Part my lips with blessed words,*
> *Stir up my heart and banish out of it all spite.*
> *I look up to the Son of the Nurse,*
> *Her one and only Son of Mercy,*
> *For He it is who has so excellently redeemed us*
> *And His we are whether we live or die.*[29]

Then, as the church is sighted, people would pray:

> *Blessed is the House of God*
> *And I myself greet Him*
> *Where He is with the Twelve Apostles.*
> *May the Son of God bless us.*
> *Blessed are you, O holy Father,*
> *Blessed are you, O temple of the Holy Spirit,*
> *Blessed are you, O church of the Trinity.*[30]

And then, sighting the altar and cross, a further prayer:

Hail to you, O altar,
O beautiful, flowering, green cross,
Let not my soul pass you by.
May you keep me in the state of grace,
May you convert us to the right way,
May you enlarge our hearts to be filled with glory,
May you fill our eyes with tears of repentance,
May you give us our share of every Mass
That is celebrated in Rome today
And throughout the whole world. Amen.[31]

The importance of the priest in Irish history cannot be over-estimated. Priests were not set up on pedestals, but they were dearly loved because they brought Christ to the people. The Celtic people had a little poem that summed up their notion of an ideal priest:

I would like a fine, pleasant, cheerful priest,
Full of faith, charitable and kindly,
Who would have sympathy for the poor and be
*   gentle with his flock,*
But I would not like a good-for-nothing in the fair
*   livery of the Only Son.*[32]

The common sense approach to clergy by Celtic Christians can be a healing help to us today. No matter what century or time period, there have always been bad clergy. In a world touched by original sin, that should come as no surprise to us. But the good always outnumber the bad, and the Celtic Christian knew this. To pray for the priest, to understand frailty, to call a bad priest to accountability, these were normal actions for a Celtic Christian, who seldom confused the office of priesthood with the man who was currently occupying the position. The intimacy and close contact of priest and people helped keep both parishioner and priest focused on their true path in life: namely, the road to Christ, walked in as much truth and purity as was possible.

During the age of the priest hunters, Catholic life in Ireland faced its most grievous trial. Sean na'Sagart and other priest hunters during the sixteenth and seventeenth centuries killed priests outright and received payment: thirty pounds for a simple priest; fifty pounds for a bishop; forty pounds for a vicar general; fifty pounds for a Jesuit. The people hated the priest hunters. For example, Edward Tyrrell was a notorious one, and when he himself was hanged for another crime an Irish poet wrote: "Good is thy fruit O tree! The luck of thy fruit on every bough; Would that all the trees of Ireland, Were full of thy fruit every single day!" The bond between Irish clergy and laity had always been strong, but was cemented even stronger at this time.[33]

The connection between Irish Catholics, their priests, and the Apostolic See in Rome was not based on some misguided sense of Church. They saw unity and treasured it in the midst of the chaos at home. Their love for their priest occurred because they deeply understood the Mass. They knew their priests were acting *in persona Christi*, in the person of Christ.

Priest and people all had a role to play. But what was most important to everyone was the fact that Christ was visiting. Here is a welcoming prayer that people would recite just after the Consecration:

A hundred thousand welcomes to You, Body of
*   the Lord,*
You, son of her the Virgin, the brightest, most
*   adorned,*
Your death in such fashion
On the tree of the passion
Has saved Eve's race and put sin to death.

I am a poor sinner to You appealing,
Reward me not as my sins may be;
O Jesus Christ I deserve Your anger,
But turn again and show grace to me.

Jesus who bought us,
Jesus who taught us,
Jesus of the united prayer,
Do not forget us
Now nor in the hour of death.

O crucified Jesus, do not leave us,
You poured Your blood for us, O forgive us,
May the Grace of the Spirit for ever be with us,
And whatever we ask may the Son of God give us.[34]

In our modern age people scream and shout in welcome at movie stars, athletes and politicians, but rarely do they become that excited about Christ. The old Celtic Christians cried out their welcome to Christ after the Consecration, saying, "A hundred thousand welcomes, O Lord"—their version of "Christ has died. Christ is risen. Christ will come again!" They understood and appreciated what occurred at each Mass, and they serve as a sterling example to today's Catholics.

Meditation

Somewhere around the year 1200, the following sermon was preached in Ireland. It is noteworthy for how succinctly it sums up the belief in the power of the Eucharist. Read it slowly and carefully:

Holy preachers explain the Body of Christ in three ways; first: His Human Body, born of the Virgin Mary without loss of her virginity; second: the Holy Church, i.e. the perfect community of all the faithful, their head is the Savior Jesus Christ, the son of God; third: Holy Scripture, in which the pure mystery of Christ's Body and Blood is recorded.

Wherefore the question arises: Since Christ was crucified only once for us, what use is it for us to offer the sacrifice of the Body and Blood of Christ every day? This is the reason: Since we sin daily we need to be cleansed every day from these sins and furthermore we may not be allowed by the church to forget Christ's crucifixion since it is recalled every day in the sacrifice. For who, among the faithful, as [Pope] Gregory assures us, doubts that when the priest raises his voice in the sacrifice heaven opens and the choirs of angels descend and the heavenly and earthly church is united and intimately bonded?[35]

How do you view the Eucharist? Is it an encounter with God? Does the Eucharist heal you, help strengthen you? What must you do to more deeply encounter Christ in this sacrament?

Contemplation

Next time you receive the Eucharist, stay after Mass for a little while in silent communion with your Lord and Savior, Jesus Christ. The celebration of the liturgy finished, you are now going to simply bask in the presence of God. As an old man once told St. John Vianney, the Cure of Ars, "I just look at Christ, and Christ looks back at me."

Action

Three things to do: one, read the Scriptures more; two, invest in your parish more; three, receive the Eucharist and pray before the Presence of Christ in the tabernacle more. How you do this is up to you, but write down what you are planning. Don't make it too onerous. Be reasonable, and accomplish it within the month. Make all three practices part of your spiritual routine.

Conclusion

And it came to pass that Columba grew very old, and his brother monks on the island of Iona feared that the Lord would soon call their beloved abbot to his heavenly home. It was in the month of May this happened, when the ocean brings the warm taste of summer and the birds sing cheerfully with their young. Columba was going to visit the monks who were laboring on the western side of the island. Because of his advanced age, he was riding in a wagon. When he found the brothers he began to speak. "My brothers," he said. "Only last month we celebrated the great feast of Easter. It had been granted to me by the Lord that I might die then, for I do greatly wish to walk with Jesus forever. But I chose to put off a little longer the day of my departure, so that the glorious feast of Easter might not be turned into a day of sorrow." The monks grew sorrowful at these words, for now the saint himself had spoken of his death. What had merely been speculation before was now a real possibility. Columba tried to cheer them up as best he could, but finally he could only turn his face to the east and bless the island and all its inhabitants.

Only a few days later, when Mass was being celebrated, the monks saw Columba lift up his eyes to heaven and his face began to glow with a beautiful light. Columba saw an angel that day hovering above him within the walls of the church itself. The saint said to those around him, "Look! It is an angel of the Lord sent to recover something dear to God." No one knew what the angel had come for, except Columba, for whom the angel had come to summon to the court of Jesus Christ.

One week later, on Sunday, the saint was blessing the grain in the barn and he said to his brother monks, "There now, you are blessed with grain so that even though I have to depart you will have bread enough for the year." Then Diarmid, his faithful servant, came up to him and said, "Father, you sadden us with this kind of talk; how can we bear your passing away?" And Columba took the young man aside and said, "I will tell you something that no one else may know until after my death. Today is the Sabbath, the day of rest, and for me it truly is a day of rest, for it is my last day of life. At midnight, I shall go the way of my fathers, for Christ has invited me to heaven." Diarmid began to weep bitterly, and Columba comforted him as best he could.

Columba walked from the barn towards the monastery and sat with Diarmid at the base of a small hill. The day was cloudy, and the afternoon sun was failing. A mist was coming from across the ocean. It was then that hoof beats were heard, galloping, galloping, closer and closer. The saint and his servant looked to the top of the hill, and a white horse appeared and reared in greeting. The stallion shone like starlight in the gloomy mist, and then galloped down toward where the two waited. As the horse came closer, the splendid beast on the hill turned out to be none other than the old faithful white horse of Columba's that had carried the milk vessels between the cow pasture and the monastery. Slowly it walked the few paces toward Columba, and wonder of wonders, knelt and placed its head on the breast of Columba. And then, praise to God for his glorious creation, knowing that Columba was soon to die, the horse began to weep, great wet tears flowing down its face to fall in the lap of the saint. So deep was the grief of this creature that it wept aloud in great sorrow. When Diarmid saw this, he began to drive away the weeping mourner, but the saint, holding the head of the horse close to himself, forbade his servant, saying: "Let him that loves us pour out the tears of most bitter grief here upon me. Diarmid, man that you are, you knew nothing of my leaving except what I have told you. But to this gentle beast, the Creator has revealed clearly that its master is going to depart." Columba helped the horse to its feet and blessed the creature as it turned sadly away from him.

That evening around midnight, the bell began to toll for prayer. A watch was kept by the brothers around Columba, who was lying quietly on his stone bed with its stone pillow. As the bell pealed, Columba jumped up from the stone pillow where he rested his head and ran to the church, entering it before all others. Bowing his knees in prayer, he sank down beside the altar. In that moment, Diarmid saw from a distance the whole church filled inside with angelic light about the saint. Far away in Ireland, a holy man name Luguid saw a vision at that very hour. He saw the whole island of Iona lit up with the brightness of angels who were sent from heaven to bear aloft the holy soul of Columba. And in another part of Ireland, a man who later became a great monk was fishing in the valley of the river Finn. All the sky was lit by a very great pillar of fire brighter than the summer sun at noontime. And after that pillar pierced the sky darkness followed, as after the setting of the sun. Darkness had also come to the little church *on Iona, for by the time Diarmid reached the doorway, the light had faded from the chapel. "Where are you, where are you, father?" he said. And groping in the darkness, he found the saint lying before the altar. Raising him a little, and sitting down beside him, he placed the holy head upon his lap. Meanwhile all the other monks ran up with lights, and when they saw that Columba was dying they began to weep. Just then, Columba opened his eyes and his face was filled with joy and gladness for he was gazing upon the holy angels who had come to meet him. And Columba stretched out his hand, blessed his brothers, and breathed his last. Thus it was that the soul of Columba left the tabernacle of his body.*[36]

THE DEATH OF ST. COLUMBA

nyone who sets out on the journey of life learns that the road of sorrow, the way of joy runs in the shadow of the cross. As guests of the world, we know that "the road's end is our true homeland."[37] It is fitting that we end our immersion in Celtic prayer with the beautiful story of St. Columba's death. In this ancient story, all the salient features of Celtic spirituality reveal themselves. The virtue of *detachment* shows forth clearly as Columba makes it known that he must leave this earth. He loves his brothers but knows that his true home awaits elsewhere. Always he is *aware of the presence of the Divine.* The spectacular nature of his last moments sometimes overshadows the race in the dark to the chapel to spend his final time on earth in a holy space dedicated to God. His magnificent *hospitality* shines through in his love and care for his monks as he bids them farewell while they labor in the field, *making holy their work* by infusing it with the blessing of God. He demonstrates his awareness of the *sacramental nature of the world* when he enfolds his beloved weeping horse and consoles the creature in its grief. Even on his dying day, *asceticism* marks his life as he rests on the stone pillow that cradles his head in his small monastic hut. His love for *Word* and *Eucharist* is no more amply demonstrated as when, knowing himself to be dying, he heads for the church where God's Word is proclaimed and God's Body and Blood is consumed. Lying, most likely cruciform, in front of the altar, he mirrors his Savior on the Cross, forming in his own body the virtues of *salvation, judgment* and *repentance* that the Cross elicits in us. And at the moment of his death, which modern humanity fears so much and molds into an icon of loneliness, Columba experiences his *community* around him and an inexpressible *hope* in his heart as the angels came to sing him to paradise.

The story of Columba's death has endured because it encapsulates basic hopes and desires in us. Could such a thing really have happened? Can death be such a blessing? Will the angels come and sing for us when it comes time for us to leave this earth? All these questions run in our minds. But those questions did not exist for the ancient Celts, at least not in the skeptical form in which we frame them.

The pagan Celts had a robust vision of the afterlife. *Tir na nOg,* the Land of Eternal Youth, was the Isle of the Uttermost West, where the Blessed were said to dwell. It represented life as it was meant to be lived. St. Brendan himself thought he might be able to sail to it, and so began his tremendous voyage across the Atlantic. For the ancient Celts, the reward for the heroes of their legends was to reside forever in this blessed place, but "only by performing heroic deeds and overcoming seemingly superhuman odds could the hero arrive at the Otherworld and share its spoils, for the gods do not easily part with what belongs to them."[38] Death, for the pagan Celt, was not simply an end. Nor did it lead to some sort of shadowy existence, but rather to a vibrant afterlife.

Imagine when the Christians came along! Their vision of the afterlife meshed wonderfully with the Celtic world view. Now, instead of worldly heroic deeds, spiritual heroism became the ideal. In fact, the ideas of pilgrimage and penitential quests that are woven into the heart and soul of Celtic Christian spirituality have a faint echo in ancient pagan heroic quests. While heaven could not be earned, these pilgrimages and penitential disciplines prepare the soul for the Otherworld, cleansing and preparing people for the true human life that waits beyond death's door.[39] No more stingy pagan god trying to deny a person life in the next realm. Instead the Christ who conquered death welcomed all who were faithful to him. The road of sorrow, way of joy became a magnificent quest available to any person—a quest for the true prize: life eternal with Jesus Christ.

Heaven for the Celtic Christian was a wonderful ideal, something to be desired and pursued. This tremendously positive vision of the afterlife helped take away the fear of death. Death was a doorway, a passing to a new existence, not an extinction. That does not mean there was no sorrow with death. For the

Celtic Christian the physical act of dying was often brutal, painful and terrible, but death itself was a blessing. To have to say goodbye to a loved one was truly terrible, but it was not forever. The Celtic Christian, perhaps more than most Christians, realized that loved ones would be reunited after death if they were faithful to Christ. Death has no power, no victory, no sting—Christ saw to that. In a world where many doubt the possibility of human existence after death, the Celtic vision of the afterlife is a strengthening support.

The Christian believes that we were never meant to be mere sparks of existence—flaming for a brief moment and then extinguished forever. Our identities continue on into the afterlife. Thus, there is no coming back for a second chance, and reincarnation is not part of our belief system. The resurrection of the body, which is the keystone of our belief on the afterlife, precludes this. The body, of course, is more than just the flesh we have. After all, scientists tell us that our body is recycled about every six months, so it's not so difficult to believe that the new, glorified body we get in the afterlife is different from the one we have now, yet holding all that is essential to who and what we are. If we are to continue to exist body and soul, then the afterlife must accommodate that mode of life.

This is why the ancient Celts had little difficulty embracing Christianity. When they heard Christians emphasizing the afterlife and speaking of it as Jesus did—as a banquet—they grabbed onto it with all the gusto they could manage. Christianity was not something new for them but rather the fulfillment of what they had always thought. The pagan Celts, soon to be Christian, saw the resurrected Christ as a familiar friend, the Chief of Chiefs, the

King of all High Kings, the one who ruled the blessed land of *Tir na nOg*.

This vibrant vision of the afterlife galvanized the Celts into heroic deeds of spiritual greatness. The characteristics they showed in their lives on earth can galvanize all of us into a renewed, more passionate Christian faith. Spirituality for the Celts was meant to unite this world with the next. It was meant to be an enjoyable and intimate part of daily life. If we walk the road of sorrow, the way of joy, we should do so in the shadow of the Cross, with Christ as our companion and guide. We will finally arrive at our true home, that place we call heaven but what any true Celtic Christian would call "the Isle of the Uttermost West, where the Blessed are said to dwell."

Meditation

On a blank sheet of paper, write "Heaven" at the top, and then fill the page with how you think the afterlife will truly be. Use just one page, but fill it with as much detail as you can. What will heaven look like? Who will be there? What will you do "all day"? On the reverse side, write down the ten things you need to focus on in *this* life to make the afterlife a real possibility for you. Of course, if you think you deserve heaven just as you are, this will seem a useless exercise. But I hope that this book has helped you to see that we all have to journey on the road to heaven.

Contemplation

Use this passage by St. Augustine, his closing words of his great work *The City of God*, as a jump start to some quality silent time with God. To truly contemplate is to let a little bit of heaven into one's soul. Read these words, and then sit in the presence of God and allow the Creator to speak to you.

The end will not be an evening, but the Lord's Day...which is to last for ever, a day consecrated by the resurrection of Christ, foreshadowing the eternal rest not only of the spirit but of the body also. There we shall be still and see; we shall see and we shall love; we shall love and we shall praise. Behold what will be, in the end, without end! For what is our end but to reach that kingdom which has no end?

St. Augustine, City of God, Book XXII[40]

Action

Use the virtues in each chapter of this book as a checklist for the next month to see how you are living the teachings of Jesus Christ. Use the list at the end of each day to examine your conscience. Then read the blessing below before you go to sleep.

God's blessing be yours
   And well may it befall you;
Christ's blessing be yours
   And well be you entreated;
Spirit's blessing be yours,
   And well spend you your lives.
Each day that you rise up,
   Each night that you lie down.[41]

Endnotes

[1] For more detail on the life of St. Columbanus see: Tomas O
Fiach, *Columbanus In His Own Words* (Dublin: Veritas, 1990).

[2] All biblical quotations are taken from the New Revised Standard
Version of the Bible.

[3] This is a tenth century poem attributed to St. Manchon or Man-
teith, an abbot of the 6th century in Ireland. This translation is
taken from Pat Robson, *The Celtic Heart: An Anthology Of
Prayers And Poems In The Celtic Tradition (London: Fount
Harper Collins, 1998),* pp. 162-63.

[4] Natalie Angier, "Confessions of a Lonely Atheist," *New York
Times Magazine* (January 14, 2001: pp.35-38).

[5] Translation from the Gaelic by Francis Cecil Alexander.

[6] This story is retold by the author from ancient sources.

[7] John J. O'Riordain, C.SS.R., *Irish Catholic Spirituality: Celtic
and Roman* (Dublin: The Columba Press, 1998), p. 30.

[8] From the Gaelic.

[9] John J. O'Riordain, C.SS.R., *Irish Catholic Spirituality: Celtic
and Roman* (Dublin: The Columba Press, 1998) p. 31.

[10] B. Kennelly, ed., *The Penguin Book of Irish Verse* (Middlesex:
Penguin, 1970), II, p. 19.

[11] O'Riordain, p. 32.

[12] Clarence Enzler, *Everyone's Way Of The Cross* (Notre Dame:
Ave Maria Press, 2000).

[13] The simple prayers of face-washing and bed-making can be
found in Esther de Waal's *A World Made Whole: Rediscovering
the Celtic Tradition* (London: Harper Collins, 1991), p. 19. The

"Fisherman's Prayer" and the "Smooring Blessing" come from Alexander Carmichael's collection of Celtic prayers, *Carmina Gadelica*, vol. 1.

[14] This distinction was made popular by one of the well-known Scripture commentator William Barclay, a Scottish Presbyterian minister. See his commentary on Hebrews in *The Daily Study Bible Series (Philadelphia:Westminster Press, 1975)*.

[15] Daphne Pouchin Mould, *The Celtic Saints* (New York: MacMillan Company, 1956) pp. 85-86.

[16] Barclay, *Commentary on Hebrews 12:1-4.*

[17] O'Riordain, p. 36.

[18] Adapted and retold from ancient sources. A good collection of the stories of this saint can be found in Eileen Dunlop, *Tales of St. Columba (Swords, Ireland: Poolbeg Press Ltd., 1992)*.

[19] Pope John Paul II, *Veritatis Splendor, 4.*

[20] Ibid.

[21] Mould, p. 110

[22] O'Riordan, p.37.

[23] Ibid, pp. 37-38.

[24] This is a compilation of ancient stories. A version of this can be found in Christopher Bamford and William Parker Marsh, eds., *Celtic Christianity: Ecology and Holiness* (Hudson, New York: The Lindisfarne Press, 1987), pp. 84-86.

[25] Ancient prayer adapted by the author from Alexander Carmichael, *Carmina Gadelica*. An easy-to-use edition is published from Floris Books, Edinburgh, 1992. This prayer can be found as #18.

[26] This version in praise of St. Brigid is adapted from *The Lives of the Saints* in the ancient *Book of Lismore*. It can be found in

Christopher Bamford and William Parker Marsh, eds., *Celtic Christianity: Ecology and Holiness* (Hudson, New York: The Lindisfarne Press, 1987), pp. 63-69.

[27] In the regions around Ballintubber Abbey in the west of Ireland, the story of Sean na'Sagart is well known. Under the tree that breaks his grave, the local people who give the abbey tour tell this story under various forms.

[28] Peter O'Dwyer, O. Carm., *Towards a History of Irish Spirituality* (Dublin: The Columba Press, 1995), p. 36.

[29] O'Riordan, p. 88 (taken from Fr. Diarmid O'Laoghaire, *Our Mass Our Life*, p. 8, Dublin: Messenger, 1968).

[30] Ibid.

[31] Ibid.

[32] O'Riordan, p. 90, quoting O'Laoghaire, pp. 16-17.

[33] O'Riordan, pp. 92-95.

[34] O'Riordan, p. 90 taken from O'Laoghaire, p. 27.

[35] O'Dwyer, O. Carm., Ibid., p. 116-117, quoting Frederic Mac Donncha, OFM, "Seanmoireacht in Eirinn, o 1000 go 1200, *An Leann Eaglasta 1000-1200 (eag. M. Mac Conmara MSC) (Ath Cliath, 1982) 72-95.*

[36] Adaptations from Adamnan's "Chronicle of Columba's Life."

[37] St. Columbanus, Sermon 8

[38] Sean O'Duinn, "The Cult of the Dead in Early Irish (Celtic) Spirituality," in *Celtic Threads: Exploring the Wisdom of Our Heritage*, ed. by Padraigin Clancy (Dublin: Veritas, 1999), p. 69.

[39] Ibid.

[40] Augustine, *City of God*, ed. David Knowles (Middlesex, England: Penguin Books, 1972).

[41] Carmichael, *Carmina Gadelica*, III, 211.

Also Available

A Contemporary Celtic Prayer Book
WILLIAM JOHN FITZGERALD
Foreword by JOYCE RUPP
A Contemporary Celtic Prayer Book follows the themes of Celtic spirituality and interweaves common daily activities with the imminent presence of divinity. This beautiful prayer book captures the flavor of traditional Celtic spirituality with a simplified Liturgy of the Hours and a treasury of Celtic prayers, blessings and rituals.
160 pages, paperback, $9.95

Hidden Presence
Twelve Blessings That Transformed Sorrow or Loss
Edited by GREGORY F. AUGUSTINE PIERCE
In this collection of twelve inspiring true stories, each author recalls a very real benefit gained from a tragedy, failure, illness or disaster. Out of these horrible events they reveal how they came to realize the Christian belief that grace can flow from sadness. Authors include Irish Americans: Joyce Rupp, Patrick Hannon, Patrick T. Reardon, James Behrens and other outstanding contemporary writers.
178 pages, hardcover, $17.95

Christmas Presence
Twelve Gifts That Were More Than They Seemed
Edited by GREGORY F. AUGUSTINE PIERCE
This award-winning book contains twelve stories exploring how the true spirit of Christmas—the presence of the divine in the world—can be experienced in the gifts we give and receive in the holiday season. Each author recalls a special Christmas gift and how it evoked priceless and unforgettable emotions. Authors include Irish Americans: John Shea, Tom McGrath, Patrick Hannon, Patrick T. Reardon and other accomplished authors.
160 pages, hardcover, $17.95